NATURAL RESOURCES

Energy

NATURAL RESOURCES

AGRICULTURE
ANIMALS
ENERGY
FORESTS
LANDS
MINERALS
PLANTS
WATER AND ATMOSPHERE

ENERGY

POWERING THE PAST, PRESENT, AND FUTURE

Julie Kerr Casper, Ph.D.

CHELSEA HOUSE
PUBLISHERS
An imprint of Infobase Publishing

Energy

Chelsea House
An imprint of Infobase Publishing
132 West 31st Street
New York, NY 10001

Library of Congress Cataloging-in-Publication Data

Casper, Julie Kerr.
 Energy : powering the past, present, and future / Julie Kerr Casper.
  p. cm. — (Natural resources)
 Includes bibliographical references and index.
 ISBN-10: 0-8160-6354-0 (hardcover)
 ISBN-13: 978-0-8160-6354-3
 1. Power resources-Juvenile literature. I. Title. II. Series.

TJ163.23.C37 2007
333.79—dc22   2006034847

Chelsea House books are available at special discounts when purchased in bulk quantities for businesses, associations, institutions, or sales promotions. Please call our Special Sales Department in New York at (212) 967-8800 or (800) 322-8755.

You can find Chelsea House on the World Wide Web at http://www.chelseahouse.com

Text design by Erik Lindstrom
Cover design by Ben Peterson

Printed in the United States of America

Bang NMSG 10 9 8 7 6 5 4 3 2 1

This book is printed on acid-free paper.

All links and Web addresses were checked and verified to be correct at the time of publication. Because of the dynamic nature of the Web, some addresses and links may have changed since publication and may no longer be valid.

CONTENTS

Mankind did not weave the web of life.
We are but one strand in it. Whatever we
do to the web, we do to ourselves . . .
All things are bound together.

—Chief Seattle

The Earth has been blessed with an abundant supply of natural resources. Natural resources are those elements that exist on the planet for the use and benefit of all living things. Scientists commonly divide them down into distinct groups for the purposes of studying them. These groups include agricultural resources, plants, animals, energy sources, landscapes, forests, minerals, and water and atmospheric resources.

One thing we humans have learned is that many of the important resources we have come to depend on are not renewable. *Nonrenewable* means that once a resource is depleted it is gone forever. The fossil fuel that gasoline is produced from is an example of a nonrenewable resource. There is only a finite supply, and once it is used up, that is the end of it.

While living things such as animals are typically considered renewable resources, meaning they can potentially be replenished, animals hunted to extinction become nonrenewable resources. As we know from past evidence, the extinctions of the dinosaurs, the woolly mammoth, and the saber-toothed tiger were complete. Sometimes, extinctions like this may be caused by natural factors, such as climate change, drought, or flood, but many extinctions are caused by the activities of humans.

Overhunting caused the extinction of the passenger pigeon, which was once plentiful throughout North America. The bald eagle was hunted to the brink of extinction before it became a protected species, and African elephants are currently threatened with extinction because they are still being hunted for their ivory tusks. Overhunting is only one potential threat, though. Humans are also responsible for habitat loss. When humans change land use and convert an animal's habitat to a city, this destroys the animal's living space and food sources and promotes its endangerment.

Plants can also be endangered or become extinct. An important issue facing us today is the destruction of the Earth's tropical rain forests. Scientists believe there may be medicinal value in many plant species that have not been discovered yet. Therefore, destroying a plant species could be destroying a medical benefit for the future.

Because of human impact and influence all around the Earth, it is important to understand our natural resources, protect them, use them wisely, and plan for future generations. The environment—land, soil, water, plants, minerals, and animals—is a marvelously complex and dynamic system that often changes in ways too subtle to perceive. Today, we have enlarged our vision of the landscape with which we interact. Farmers manage larger units of land, which makes their job more complex. People travel greater distances more frequently. Even when they stay at home, they experience and affect a larger share of the world through electronic communications and economic activities- and natural resources have made these advancements possible.

The pace of change in our society has accelerated as well. New technologies are always being developed. Many people no longer spend all their time focused in one place or using things in traditional ways. People now move from one place to another and are constantly developing and using new and different resources.

A sustainable society requires a sustainable environment. Because of this, we must think of natural resources in new ways. Today, more than ever, we must dedicate our efforts to conserve the land. We still live in a beautiful, largely natural world, but that world is quickly changing. World population growth and our desire to live comfortably are exerting pressures on our soil, air, water, and other natural resources. As we destroy and fragment natural habitats, we continue to push nonhuman life into ever-smaller pockets. Today, we run the risk of those places becoming isolated islands on a domesticated landscape.

In order to be responsible caretakers of the planet, it is important to realize that we humans have a partnership with the Earth and the other life that shares the planet with us. This series presents a refreshing and informative way to view the Earth's natural resources. *Agriculture: The Food We Grow and Animals We Raise* looks at agricultural resources to see how responsible conservation, such as caring for the soil, will give us continued food to feed growing populations. *Plants: Life From the Earth* examines the multitude of plants that exist and the role they play in biodiversity. The use of plants in medicines and in other products that people use every day is also covered.

In *Animals: Creatures That Roam the Planet,* the series focuses on the diverse species of animals that live on the planet, including the important roles they have played in the advancement of civilization. This book in the series also looks at habitat destruction, exotic species, animals that are considered in danger of extinction, and how people can help to keep the environment intact.

Next, in *Energy: Powering the Past, Present, and Future,* the series explores the Earth's energy resources—such as renewable power from water, ocean energy, solar energy, wind energy, and biofuels; and non-renewable sources from oil shale, tar sands, and fossil fuels. In addition, the future of energy and high-tech inventions on the horizon are also explored.

In *Lands: Taming the Wilds,* the series addresses the land and how civilizations have been able to tame deserts, mountains, arctic regions, forests, wetlands, and floodplains. The effects that our actions can have on the landscape for years to come are also explored. In *Forests: More Than Just Trees,* the series examines the Earth's forested areas and how unique and important these areas are to medicine, construction, recreation, and commercial products. The effects of deforestation, pest outbreaks, and wildfires—and how these can impact people for generations to come—are also addressed.

In *Minerals: Gifts From the Earth,* the bounty of minerals in the Earth and the discoveries scientists have made about them are examined. Moreover, this book in the series gives an overview of the critical part minerals play in many common activities and how they affect our lives every day.

Finally, in *Water and Atmosphere: The Lifeblood of Natural Systems,* the series looks at water and atmospheric resources to find out just how these resources are the lifeblood of the natural system—from drinking water, food production, and nutrient storage to recreational values. Drought, sea-level rise, soil management, coastal development, the effects of air and water pollution, and deep-sea exploration and what it holds for the future are also explored.

The reader will learn the wisdom of recycling, reducing, and reusing our natural resources, as well as discover many simple things that can be done to protect the environment. Practical approaches such as not leaving the water running while brushing your teeth, turning the lights off when leaving a room, using reusable cloth bags to transport groceries, building a backyard wildlife refuge, planting a tree, forming a carpool, or starting a local neighborhood recycling program are all explored.

Everybody is somebody's neighbor, and shared responsibility is the key to a healthy environment. The cheapest—and most effective—conservation comes from working with nature. This series presents things that people can do for the environment now and the important role we all can play for the future. As a wise Native-American saying goes, "We do not inherit the Earth from our ancestors—we borrow it from our children."

ACKNOWLEDGMENTS

I would like to thank all the government agencies currently involved in energy research, development, and conservation—in particular, the U.S. Department of Energy and the U.S. National Renewable Energy Laboratory for their suggestions, comments, and assistance. Thanks also goes out to all the dedicated researchers across the country at various universities and other private research institutions who spend countless hours researching and experimenting with new technologies in energy management. A special thanks also to Andrea Knopp (Utah Transit Authority), Jerome Cooke (Department of Energy), Helen Criares (Department of Energy), Vikki Kourkouliotis (National Renewable Energy Laboratory), and Nature's Images, LLC, for their contributions in the acquisition of the wonderful photography in this volume.

Of all the Earth's precious resources, no other resource has contributed to the development and advancement of civilization quite like energy has. The rapid technological developments that have occurred over the past two decades alone have had a tremendous effect on our quality of life. With new sources of energy being tapped daily, the future is limited only by our imaginations.

INTRODUCTION

Energy is essential to life. Living creatures draw on energy flowing through the environment and convert it to forms they can use. The most fundamental energy flow for living creatures is the energy of sunlight, and the most important conversion is the act of biological primary production, in which plants and sea-dwelling phytoplankton convert sunlight into biomass by photosynthesis. The Earth's web of life—including human beings—rests on this foundation.

Over thousands of years, humans have found ways to extend and expand their energy harvest: first by harnessing draft animals and later by inventing machines to tap the power of wind and water. Industrialization, which triggered the development of the modern world, was enabled by the widespread and intensive use of fossil fuels. This development freed human society from the limitations of natural energy flows by discovering and utilizing the Earth's vast stores of coal, oil, and natural gas. These resources greatly multiplied the rate at which energy could be used. The result was one of the most profound social transformations in history.

This volume in the Natural Resources series looks at energy sources and how these critical resources have powered the past, power the present, and will continue to power the future.

Chapter 1 defines energy resources and the natural mechanisms in the Earth that have allowed them to form. It presents the principal types of energy and where they are found, as well as basic energy concepts, such as how energy is measured and converted from one form to another.

Chapter 2 examines the history of energy development, such as how humans' need and their development of energy have caused specific trends in civilization. It looks at the key inventions—the milestones—

that allowed us to arrive at the technical level society is at today. It focuses on the great Industrial Revolution and how it triggered the development of the modern world.

Chapter 3 looks at these various energy resources and their characteristics, such as whether they are renewable or nonrenewable. It focuses on renewable energy sources, such as solar energy, wind energy, hydropower, geothermal energy, bioenergy and biofuels, ocean energy, hydrogen energy, and nuclear power. It also identifies and defines nonrenewable energy sources, such as fossil fuels, coal, uranium, oil shale, and tar sands. It defines what alternative energy is and what is meant by "green energy." It also looks at synthetic products currently being used as energy sources and the purpose and utility of hybrid systems.

Chapter 4 focuses on the development of energy resources and their worldwide impacts. It discusses humans' need for power, the advancement of lifestyles, and the consequences due to energy development, as well as the development of military applications that have—and most likely will continue to have—a significant effect on our lives each day.

Chapter 5 then deals with the uses and impacts of energy. It looks at applications, environmental issues, human health issues, and conflicts that arise with wildlife habitats during energy exploration and utilization.

Chapter 6 relays the importance of energy. It explores the many goods and services we receive from the development of energy resources, from plastics and fuels to synthetic materials to various medicinal products.

Chapter 7 addresses the management of energy resources and why it is critical to maintain a delicate balance in order to deal with various national and international issues. It looks at the role that politics and economics plays in many countries' access, processing, and storage issues; maintenance of resources; security issues; and vulnerability—as well as how the U.S. government is handling those challenges. It also looks at the short- and long-term effects of oil spills and the effects they have on the natural environment and wildlife. Finally, it covers various experimental and research programs, such as the FreedomCAR and Vehicle Building Technologies Program, the Solar Energy Technologies

Program, the Geothermal Technologies Program, the Hydrogen and Fuel Cells Technology Program, and many others.

Chapter 8 deals with the conservation of our precious energy resources, as well as the fundamental reasons for and benefits gained from recycling, reducing, and reusing these resources. It also discusses energy efficiency and how conservation can affect not just those on the Earth today, but also those who will live on the Earth in the future.

Finally, Chapter 9 looks at cutting-edge research happening in experimental labs today, including the discovery and development of hydrogen fuel cells and the role of synthetic materials. It also illustrates how our behavior today can have an effect on societies long into the future and why it is important that we conserve natural resources and manage them wisely.

CONCEPTS OF ENERGY RESOURCES

To put it simply, **energy** is the ability to do **work**; it is the ability to make things happen. But in reality, it does much more than that. Energy is one of our most valuable resources. This chapter addresses the types of energy resources, as well as where they are found. It also discusses the ways in which energy is measured and then introduces the concepts of renewable and nonrenewable energy resources and why they are categorized differently.

FORMS OF ENERGY

Energy exists in many forms. Some forms are easy to identify as energy. Other forms of energy cannot be seen until the energy is released. Some forms of energy, such as light and sound, carry energy from one place to another. Vibrating objects, which have **kinetic energy**, make sound. The vibrations spread through the air in waves, which carry the energy with them. Particles in the air vibrate as the sound waves go by but do not actually move along. The louder the sound, the more energy there is in the vibrations of the particles. In water—such as ocean waves—when the wave moves past, the water does not move along; it just goes up and down. Energy moves through the wave, away from where the wave was caused. The higher the wave, the more energy there is.

Light is also a form of energy. It travels in straight lines called rays. A light ray carries energy from where the light is made. There is more energy in bright light than dim light, which is why the farther away a light source is, the dimmer it looks. Light is part of the family of rays called the **electromagnetic spectrum**. The electromagnetic spectrum includes radio waves, microwaves, infrared rays, **ultraviolet** rays, and X-rays. This energy is often called radiation.

Chemical energy is the energy stored in substances. Signs of this energy are only visible when the substance takes part in a chemical reaction. For example, when a **fuel** burns, the chemical energy in it is released as heat and **light energy**. Therefore, the energy stored in a **battery** is actually chemical energy. When the battery is connected to an **electric circuit**, the energy is released as **electrical energy**. Electrical energy is a useful form of energy because it can be sent along wires and used to work in many different types of machines.

Nuclear energy is the energy stored in the **nucleus** of an **atom**. When a **nuclear reaction** occurs, energy can be released as heat and light and other radiation, such as X-rays.

When somebody moves an object, energy is used. Energy is transferred to the object. This is called mechanical energy. An object can have three types of mechanical energy—kinetic energy, **elastic energy**, and **gravitational energy**. Any object that is moving has kinetic energy. The faster an object moves and the faster it is, the more kinetic energy it has. Springs have elastic energy. This energy is stored when an object is bent, twisted, or stretched. When the object is released, it springs back into its original shape, releasing elastic energy.

When an object falls downward, it has gravitational energy because it is being pulled downward by the Earth's gravity. The higher up the object—or the heavier it is—the more gravitational energy it has.

When an object is moved upward against the force of gravity, it gains more gravitational energy. When the energy is stored within an object and can be released later, this is called **potential energy**. Physics and chemistry are the two principle scientific disciplines that study the movement, motion, actions, interactions, and reactions of materials.

Most energy is initially derived from the energy of the Sun. Once it leaves the Sun, it is converted into other forms of energy, such as the energy that contributes to the growth of plants—which in turn gives many life-forms energy in the form of food. Humans get their energy from food. It is energy from the Sun that allowed plants to grow and animals to live back in prehistoric times and that has since provided humans with energy sources in the form of **oil**, gas, and **coal**—commonly called **fossil fuels**.

The Sun also provides the mechanisms that drive the **water cycle**, allowing humans to tap into the **power** of moving water to generate electricity. It also provides the power to create wind energy—another form of energy used to generate electricity.

When energy is expended, it is converted into other forms. For example, the chemical energy of gasoline is converted into movement energy as it powers cars, trucks, airplanes, lawnmowers, weed eaters,

Major Types of Energy

Kinetic energy	Potential energy
Electrical energy	Chemical energy
Radiant energy	Stored mechanical energy
Thermal energy	Nuclear energy
Motion energy	Gravitational energy
Sound energy	

leaf blowers, motorcycles, and many other objects that are powered by an engine. Lighting fixtures convert electrical energy into light energy. Brakes on a car convert movement energy into heat energy. Stereos convert electrical energy into **sound energy**. When humans move, work, and play sports, they are converting the chemical energy derived from food to movement energy.

When energy is used in its various forms and then converted to other forms, some of the energy is converted into heat energy. When heat energy is used—such as in a furnace—it is usable energy. When it is not used, however, it is wasted energy. An example of wasted energy is the heat given off from a truck's engine during and after it has been running. The higher the efficiency of a system, the less waste (usually heat) it will produce.

In order to change the form of energy, an **energy converter** must be used. Energy converters range from simple to complex. The blades of a waterwheel are a simple form of energy converter that uses the energy of falling water to turn the huge wheel. The turning wheel then does the work. Waterwheels can operate many types of machinery—and have for hundreds of years worldwide—such as a mill, which grinds grain into flour. Steam, gasoline, and electrical engines are examples of more complex converters. These can make machines work or make vehicles move. Through the use of converters, energy can be changed into mechanical or electrical

Energy From the Sun

The **heat energy** from the Sun that reaches the Earth is only one-thousandth of one-millionth of the heat produced by the Sun. The Sun is about 93 million miles (150 million kilometers) away from the Earth. If it was closer, the weather would be too hot for life, and everything would dry up and be burned. If the Sun was farther away, the climate would be too cold for life to exist, and the Earth would be covered with a layer of ice.

The Solar Two power plant uses heliostats or motorized mirrors to track the Sun and continuously concentrate sunlight onto a receiver near the top of the central tower. The tower is filled with a molten salt mixture that collects and stores enough thermal energy to drive a steam turbine that produces electricity sufficient to power 10,000 homes. *(Courtesy of U.S. Department of Energy)*

energy. Electrical energy supplies the heat, light, and power humans need every day. Mechanical energy moves machines and other objects.

Many commonly used systems lose up to 40% of their energy as wasted heat. Humans are continually trying to solve this problem through technology. Today, many converters can change energy from different sources directly into electrical energy with no resulting heat loss. The solar battery is an example of this type of converter.

Sources of energy are not always close to where they are needed. This means that energy has to be transported from one place to another.

Because energy is central to humans' lives, enormous amounts are transported every day—much of it in the form of stored energy, or fuel.

The three principal fuels used for energy—oil, gas, and coal—are bulky and have to be transported as inexpensively as possible in order to keep the energy source affordable. Oil and gas can be moved by several methods through pipelines and by supertankers. A well-known example of oil being transported through a pipeline is the oil fields in northern Alaska. The fields are remote, and the subsequent lack of roadways and the harsh climate make it difficult to gain access by any other way than by pipeline. The pipe is raised up on stilts above ground for much of its journey. It cannot be buried because the ground is frozen underneath and the surface only thaws during the summer months, making it dangerous to bury the pipeline. The oil is kept moving at all times by pumps to keep it from freezing in the pipe.

Because coal is a solid, transporting it requires ship, train, or truck. Coal is often transported from the coal mine to a coal-using **power station**. Electricity, on the other hand, can be transported for long distances cheaply by using thick power cables suspended from tall **pylons** (steel towers). **Natural gas** is very bulky, and it is only convenient to transport it as a gas through pipelines. Natural gas can also be cooled under pressure, converting it into a liquid. This type of gas can be used in camping stoves and barbecues.

Because there are many different kinds of energy—such as **solar energy**, chemical energy, electrical energy, mechanical energy, and nuclear energy—it is important to understand that any form of energy can be changed into other forms. No matter what form energy takes, all are equal. An example of this is turning on a flashlight. As soon as the switch is flicked, the battery's chemical energy has instantly been changed into light energy. When a television is turned on, it converts electrical energy into light and sound energy. When a tree is cut with a wood saw, mechanical energy is changed into thermal energy.

Another important aspect about energy is that it never disappears. Although it can change forms, it is never created and never destroyed. It is only converted from one form to another. Science is based on

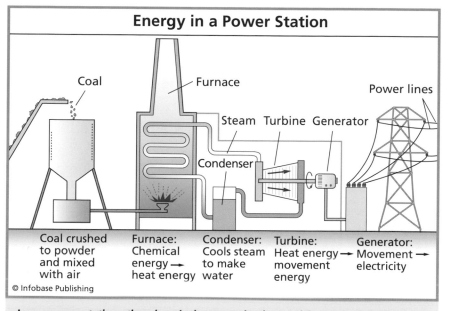

Energy in a Power Station

Coal

Furnace

Power lines

Steam Turbine Generator

Condenser

| Coal crushed to powder and mixed with air | Furnace: Chemical energy → heat energy | Condenser: Cools steam to make water | Turbine: Heat energy → movement energy | Generator: Movement → electricity |

© Infobase Publishing

In a power station, the chemical energy in the coal is converted into heat energy. The steam is cooled into water and the turbine converts the heat energy into kinetic energy. The generator takes the kinetic energy and changes it into electrical energy.

this fact—no energy can be made without using an equal amount of another energy form.

LOCATIONS OF ENERGY SOURCES

During the twentieth century, energy has become much more easily available. Most energy comes from burning fossil fuels (oil, gas, and coal). These resources are only found in certain geologic formations. Fossil fuels were formed millions of years ago from vegetative matter and animal remains (fossils) that collected and decayed in swamp-like conditions. Over the eons of time, this material was compacted, overlaid with sedimentary rock, and put under great pressure from the geologic processes of the Earth. This is where the term *fossil fuels* came from—they are the fuels from the fossils of dead plants and animals.

Subsequently, only specific areas of the world have deposits of **petroleum** (oil). These deposits were formed only under specific geologic conditions in specific locations on Earth. According to the U.S. Department of Energy, the world's top five crude-oil-producing countries are:

- Saudi Arabia
- Russia
- United States
- Iran
- China

Wind energy is one way of producing clean, renewable electricity. **Wind power plants**, or **wind farms** as they are sometimes called, are clusters of wind machines used to produce electricity. Wind power plants need to be built in areas where there is a consistent wind source. Because wind speed increases with altitude and over open areas with no windbreaks, good sites for wind plants are the tops of smooth, rounded hills; open plains; shorelines; and mountain gaps that funnel wind. In some geographic areas, the wind blows more on a seasonal basis, which is another factor to consider when deciding on the location to construct a wind tower.

Hydropower is also limited in terms of where it can be produced. Because the source of hydropower is water, hydroelectric power plants must be located on a water source. Therefore, it wasn't until the technology to transmit electricity over long distances was developed that hydropower became widely used.

Geothermal energy is energy from the Earth's core. In a few places, heat from the Earth can be collected. Usually, engineers try to collect this heat from these rare places where the Earth's crust has trapped steam and hot water by drilling into the crust and allowing the heat to escape, either as steam or as very hot water. Pipes carry the hot water to a plant where some of the steam is allowed to "flash," or separate, from the water. That steam then turns a turbine

Geothermal energy is a site-specific form of energy. Where the geologic conditions are right, the Earth releases immense amounts of heat. This energy can be harnessed and converted into electricity. This plant is located in Sonoma and Lake Counties, California, and is called the Geysers Complex. It is the only commercial geothermal power plant in the United States. *(Courtesy of U.S. Department of Energy)*

generator to make electricity. Energy generation from geothermal sources is "site specific," meaning it is only possible in a few places under unique geologic conditions. There are several geothermal areas in the United States. Some European countries also use geothermal energy. The capital of Iceland—Reykjavik—is heated mostly by geothermal energy.

UNITS OF MEASUREMENT

It is often useful to know how much energy is being changed from one form to another. For example, natural gas companies need to have a way to measure the fuel demands of their customers so they can provide enough natural gas when it is most needed.

In most scientific experiments, there is some form of energy measurement. A **meter** is an instrument that measures energy—such as the power and gas meters located on the sides of houses—and the standard unit of energy in the metric system is called a **joule** (J).

Energy can be measured in many different units. A calorie is defined as the amount of heat energy needed to raise the **temperature** of 2.2 pounds (1 kilogram) of water by 1.8°F (1°C). Power is simply the rate at which the energy is changed.

Energy can also be measured in units called foot-pounds. One foot-pound is the amount of work done in moving an object one foot against a 1-pound force. Therefore, if a 4-pound weight is lifted 6 feet off the ground, it is using 24 foot-pounds of energy.

Horsepower is another measurement that describes energy. But it is a measure of power, not of energy itself. Power is not the same as energy. Energy is the ability to do work. Power is a measure of how

Measuring Energy

Energy is measured in joules, which are very small amounts of energy. A mug of hot chocolate cooling down at room temperature will release about 100,000 joules. The calorie is an old-fashioned unit often used to measure the energy contained in food. A slice of bread contains about 70 calories. One calorie equals about 4,000 joules. Power is the rate at which energy is given off or used, and it is measured in watts. The use of 1 joule of energy every second is 1 watt. A 60-watt lightbulb uses 60 joules of energy every second to give off heat and light.

Btu Content of Common Types of Energy

1 barrel of crude oil (42 gallons)	5,800,000 Btu
1 gallon of gasoline	124,000 Btu
1 gallon of heating oil	139,000 Btu
1 gallon of diesel fuel	139,000 Btu
1 barrel of residual fuel oil	6,287,000 Btu
1 cubic foot of natural gas	1,026 Btu
1 gallon of propane	91,000 Btu
1 short ton of coal	20,681,000 Btu
1 kilowatt-hour of electricity	3,412 Btu

quickly it is done. Mechanical power is measured in units called *horse-power*. James Watt, a Scottish engineer, first suggested the term when working with the newly invented steam engine. When doubtful farm ers asked how many horses a steam engine could replace, this term was invented in order to make a logical comparison. Watt measured the amount of work a horse did in an eight-hour period. Many types of power are now measured in units called **watts (W)**.

Physical units reflect measures of distance, area, volume, height, weight, mass, force, impulse, and energy. Different types of energy are measured by different physical units: barrels or gallons for petroleum; cubic feet for natural gas; tons for coal; and **kilowatt-hours** for electricity. To compare different fuels, it is necessary to convert the measurements to the same units. In the United States, the unit of measure most commonly used for comparing fuels is the British Thermal Unit (Btu), which is the amount of energy required to raise the temperature of 1 pound of water 1°F. One Btu is approximately equal to the energy released in the burning of a wood match.

THE TWO CATEGORIES OF ENERGY RESOURCES

The energy that humans use every day comes from resources. Resources are broken up into two main categories—renewable and nonrenewable. Renewable resources are those that can be used or made over and over again from other resources; they are unlimited.

Most **renewable energy** comes either directly or indirectly from the Sun. Sunlight, or solar energy, can be used directly for heating and lighting homes and other buildings, for generating electricity, and for hot-water heating, solar cooling, and a variety of commercial and industrial uses.

The Sun's heat also drives the wind, whose energy is captured with wind turbines. Then, the wind and the Sun's heat cause water to evaporate. When this water vapor turns into rain or snow and flows downhill into rivers or streams, its energy can be captured using hydroelectric power.

Along with the rain and snow, sunlight causes plants to grow. The organic matter that makes up those plants is known as biomass. Biomass can be used to produce electricity, transportation fuels, or chemicals. This is called **biomass energy**.

Hydrogen can also be found in many organic compounds as well as water. It is the most abundant element on Earth, but it does not occur naturally as a gas. It is always combined with other elements, such as with oxygen, to produce water. Once separated from another element, hydrogen can be burned as a fuel or converted into electricity.

Wood is a renewable resource because more trees can be grown to make more wood. Renewable energy resources also include geothermal energy from inside the Earth.

Renewable energy, once a dream of the future, is becoming more mainstream every day. People are realizing the benefits of switching to renewable energy. From installing **solar panels** at home to using waste products to provide heat and power for communities to utility companies offering power from renewable energy sources (such as wind-power-generated electricity), the future of renewable energy sources is now a reality for many parts of the world.

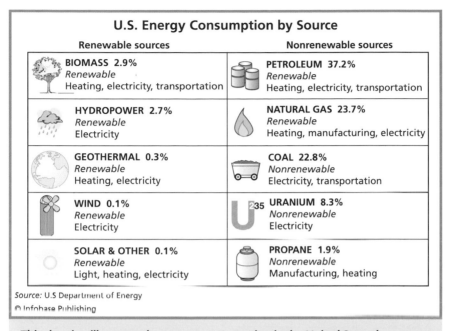

U.S. Energy Consumption by Source

Renewable sources	Nonrenewable sources
BIOMASS 2.9% *Renewable* Heating, electricity, transportation	**PETROLEUM 37.2%** *Renewable* Heating, electricity, transportation
HYDROPOWER 2.7% *Renewable* Electricity	**NATURAL GAS 23.7%** *Renewable* Heating, manufacturing, electricity
GEOTHERMAL 0.3% *Renewable* Heating, electricity	**COAL 22.8%** *Nonrenewable* Electricity, transportation
WIND 0.1% *Renewable* Electricity	**URANIUM 8.3%** *Nonrenewable* Electricity
SOLAR & OTHER 0.1% *Renewable* Light, heating, electricity	**PROPANE 1.9%** *Nonrenewable* Manufacturing, heating

Source: U.S Department of Energy
© Infobase Publishing

This drawing illustrates the energy consumption in the United States by source. Petroleum, natural gas, and coal are still the most widely used; followed by nuclear (uranium), biomass, hydropower, propane, geothermal, wind, and solar energy.

Nonrenewable resources are those energy sources that humans are using up and cannot recreate in a short period of time. Although the biological and geologic processes are still occurring today as they were in prehistoric times, the formation of these nonrenewable resources takes millions of years; therefore, humans in their lifetimes will not benefit from these "future" resources. Nonrenewable energy sources are commonly described as those resources that cannot be replaced within a human lifetime. These energy resources include oil, natural gas, and coal. Another nonrenewable resource is the element uranium, whose atoms are split (through a process called nuclear **fission**) to create heat and electricity.

Humans use all these energy sources to generate the electricity needed for homes, businesses, schools, churches, and factories.

Electricity enables humans to have computers, lights, refrigerators, washing machines, microwaves, vacuums, stereos, televisions, air conditioners, curling irons, blow driers, alarm clocks, as well as many other things.

Humans use energy to operate their cars and other machinery. Most gasoline is made from oil, although there are other fuels available from corn (called ethanol). Propane—made from oil and natural gas—is used to cook on outdoor grills, heat some homes, and fly hot-air balloons.

Energy is in everything. Humans use energy to accomplish many tasks. Such activities as using a computer, baking cookies, driving to the store, and sending astronauts into outer space require the use of energy. Because it is such a critical resource, not only in our daily existence but for our material progress, we need to understand the issues surrounding energy and use it wisely. If we don't, it may not be available for future generations.

THE HISTORY OF ENERGY

Beginning in ancient times, fire was discovered and put to work. This type of energy allowed primitive peoples to cook, heat their dwellings, and scare wild animals away. This chapter explores the history of the discovery and use of energy and the importance it played in the development of human civilization. It begins by looking at the historical development of different forms of energy and then examines the development of energy in the United States.

THE HISTORICAL DEVELOPMENT OF ENERGY

Humans have used fire for thousands of years—even as far back as the late Stone Age. Archaeologists have determined that cave dwellers kept their caves warm with fires that were kept continually burning. Later, humans used fire in more sophisticated ways, such as for cooking food, providing light, firing pottery, smelting **ore**, and making glass.

In ancient times, people used the energy stored in their own muscles to do work, such as hunting, gathering food, and building shelter. Simple tools were invented to assist in these efforts. The earliest tools were made of wood. Later, they were made from metal. Human power was also used to make the first boats and then to propel them by using poles and oars.

Some of the work was very difficult to do with just human power, so people turned to animals such as oxen. Animals supplied the energy necessary to complete several tasks: They provided transportation, helped move heavy goods from one place to another, and were used to plow fields for cultivation and pump water for irrigation. People have used animals to pull plows for thousands of years; the first plows can be traced back to Mesopotamia in 4000 B.C.

Wind Energy

Wind is another usable energy source that can be traced back thousands of years. The first mechanical device that was built to use the wind as a source of power was the sailboat. Sailboats and larger sailing ships provided a critical service because they allowed humans to begin exploring and trading with other civilizations. For this, harbors were built, creating towns and cities along coastlines around the world.

The first sailing ships had simple square sails that simply carried them in the direction the wind blew. It was Arab sailors who discovered how to sail into the wind using a triangular sail called the lateen—similar to the triangular sails that are still used today.

The first machine designed to use wind power to do work on land was the **windmill**, which was invented in the seventh century in Persia (now Iran). This new technology then spread to the Middle East and other countries such as India and China. The windmill was one of the first large-scale inventions designed to make peoples' workloads easier. Windmills were initially used to grind grain between heavy millstones to make flour. They were also used to pump water from rivers to irrigate crops. In sawmills, people used the motion of the shaft to run a saw, which slid up and down to slice rough logs into pieces of lumber.

Windmills were not built in Europe until the twelfth century. The Europeans used them to generate power and invented a new type of mill, called the post mill. A center post grounded this type of windmill, and the whole building turned around the center post so that the sails always faced into the wind. The stationary windmill—where only the top of the structure in which the sails were mounted turned into the wind—followed this.

Wind-powered grain mills and sawmills were replaced by more efficient machinery in the early 1900s. Some farmers still use windmills today, however, to pump water and drain flooded areas and to pull up underground water for irrigating crops. Today, high-powered windmills, called wind turbine generators, are used to make electricity.

Solar Energy

Solar energy has also been used since ancient times. The Greeks and Romans were among the first civilizations to use solar energy. They built their homes and other buildings facing south in order to take advantage of the Sun's strongest rays.

The American Indians also considered the sun when they built their dwellings. They built their structures of thick clay, which is able to absorb and hold heat from the Sun. People then learned to use the Sun to power machinery. Solar pumps and furnaces existed in the 1700s. By the 1800s, inventors were working with solar steam engines. Today, scientists continue to work with solar energy to find better ways of gathering and storing the sun's energy.

Fossil Fuels

It has been documented that the Chinese were using coal as early as 1000 B.C. to bake porcelain. The ancient Greeks also wrote about it in their history. In the Western countries, many of the forests had been destroyed by the 1100s to build houses and ships. Wood to heat houses became expensive, so people began looking for alternate ways to provide heat to their homes.

By the 1600s, coal had grown in popularity as a heating source. It was also used in breweries, glassmaking, brick making, and many other businesses. Coal continued to grow in popularity. Originally, it was mined from shallow near-surface deposits. As this coal was used, miners began building mine shafts in order to go deeper into the ground where many coal deposits existed.

Coal mining was very hazardous. Shafts and tunnels had to be supported by beams. There was also the constant danger of cave-ins, explosions, or fires. By the beginning of the 1700s, coal was used in tall furnaces. This marked the beginning of the Industrial Revolution. England had many coal deposits, and during that time, it became a very wealthy nation because of this. With the invention of the steam engine, the demand for coal further increased. Coal is the energy source that significantly changed civilization and triggered the development of the modern world.

People have used petroleum since at least 3000 B.C. Mesopotamians used "rock oil" in architectural adhesives, ship caulks, medicines, and roads. Two thousand years ago, the Chinese **refined** crude oil for use in lamps and in heating homes.

In the past, petroleum was collected in small containers from where it oozed from the ground. In America, the Indians, doctors, and pharmacists used it as a form of medicine. For example, the Indians had used it for hundreds of years to treat skin sicknesses and breathing difficulties.

People then began to find other uses for petroleum. Eventually, it replaced whale oil for lighting, and the oil lamp was invented. Most experts credit Edwin L. Drake with starting the oil industry on a large scale. In 1858, the Seneca Oil Company, which was interested in oil as a fuel, hired Drake to drill a well near Titusville, Pennsylvania. Drake worked with Billy Smith, a well digger, and dug one pit after another. The men used a wooden rig and a steam-run drill. Because each pit they dug was threatened with water and cave-ins, Drake ran an iron pipe deep into the ground and drilled from inside it. The pipe acted as a casing and kept Drake's path clear for drilling. About a year later, Drake and Smith had dug a well 69.5 feet (21.2 meters) deep. On August 27, 1859, the oil suddenly swept up the shaft.

Gas as an energy source was first manufactured in the late eighteenth century. Scientists discovered that gas could be produced from heating coal without using air—because of this, the gas was called coal gas.

William Murdock, a British engineer, is known as the father of the gas industry. In 1792, he was using gas to light his own home. Coal gas was first used for public lighting with gaslit streetlamps and public buildings. From there, its use spread to private homes.

In order to transport the gas, it was stored in elastic water skins that were stowed in horse-drawn wagons. A long tube fitted with a tap was put into the water skins. This controlled the dispensing of the gas. The wagon delivered the gas to individual homes by plugging the tube into the customer's tank. The tap was then opened, and straps were tightened around the water skins to force the gas from the skin into the tank. Eventually, gas was stored in cylinders, making it less cumbersome to deliver.

Gas began to be used as a fuel in other modes of transportation, as well. Trains, steamboats, and ships carried gas in bottles. As the demand for gas increased, more efficient delivery methods were experimented with, and eventually pipes were placed underground to directly deliver the gas from factory to home. By this time, gas was not only used for lighting, but for cooking and heating, as well.

Electricity

In 1802, Sir Humphrey Davy, an Englishman, invented the first electric light. He experimented with passing an electric spark between two conductors stuck in a battery. He added a small charcoal rod at the end of each conductor. His apparatus was then enclosed in a glass globe.

For the next few decades, inventors used this invention to light entire cities. Other inventors dreamed of having the electric light available in every home. They encountered many problems, however, in making this work. The power of the bulb needed to be refined, and a feasible method of delivering the light to customers had to be developed.

The American inventor Thomas A. Edison solved these problems. Through experimentation, he refined the lightbulb. A very fine carbon wire controlled the bulb's glow. His work was the model for the modern-day bulb. In 1882, Edison also developed one of the first electrical power plants that generated and distributed electricity. It made affordable electricity possible and had a profound effect on peoples' lives.

People dreamed of building the ideal engine. A Belgian electrician—Zenobe Gramme—found the solution. He and his associate, Hippolyte Fontaine, invented a special steam machine that could run two generators. A generator is a device that changes mechanical energy into electrical energy. These two inventors reasoned that if one generator quit working, the other could just replace it. But while one generator was producing electricity, the other was also in motion, working. They realized their machine was also reversible. It could change its own electrical energy into mechanical energy. This invention became the first electric motor.

The electric motor was first used as energy to power trains. It appeared in 1879 in Germany and then in England in 1887. In 1895, the electric train concept was brought to the United States.

Today, in most areas of the world, diversity and evolution of energy supplies has been the rule. In many areas, human labor, animal power, and biomass energy (wood) are still the primary sources of energy. The

Thomas Edison

Thomas Edison was born in 1847 in Milan, Ohio. Even as a young boy, Edison had an unending curiosity about the way things worked. He liked to experiment with different gadgets to see if he could make them work better. He even set up a laboratory in his house, where he conducted experiments.

He invented many objects in his laboratory. His inventions include the phonograph, the first lightbulb, and the first power plant. The power plant—called Edison's Pearl Street Power Station—opened in 1882 in New York City. It sent electricity to 85 customers and made enough power to light 5,000 lamps.

Michael Faraday

Born in 1791 to a poor family in England, Michael Faraday had an unstoppable curiosity. He became interested in the concept of energy—specifically the issue of force. He conducted many experiments on force and was able to make important discoveries concerning electricity. He eventually became a famous chemist and physicist.

He built two devices to produce electromagnetic rotation—a continuous circular motion from the circular magnetic force around a wire. In 1831, using his "induction ring," he made one of his greatest discoveries—electromagnetic induction. This is the induction, or generation, of electricity in a wire by means of the electromagnetic effect of a **current** in another wire. The induction ring was the first electric transformer. Faraday also invented the first generator. From his experiments came devices that led to the modern electric motor, generator, and transformer.

energy path the United States took is unique, as will be discussed in the next section.

DEVELOPMENT OF ENERGY IN THE UNITED STATES

The United States has always been a resource rich country, but in 1776—when the nation declared its independence from Great Britain—nearly all energy was still supplied by muscle power and fuel wood. America's huge deposits of petroleum and coal lay undiscovered and untapped. There were small amounts of coal being used to produce coke—which was used to cast cannons. The mills constructed at the time used waterpower, and ships used wind power.

Wood energy has been a significant part of the U.S. energy source since colonial times. It was the dominant energy source from the founding of the earliest colonies until the 1800s. Fuel wood use continued to grow, but chronic shortages of energy encouraged the search for other sources. During the first 30 years or so of the nineteenth century,

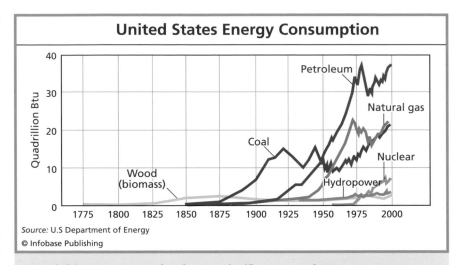

United States Energy Consumption

Quadrillion Btu

Petroleum

Natural gas

Coal

Nuclear

Wood (biomass)

Hydropower

1775 1800 1825 1850 1875 1900 1925 1950 1975 2000

Source: U.S Department of Energy

© Infobase Publishing

Wood (biomass) energy has been a significant part of U.S. energy consumption since colonial times. Fuel wood was the dominant energy source from the founding of the earliest colonies until the middle of the 1800s. Coal then became the dominant energy source; but after 1950, petroleum and natural gas have been in greater demand.

coal began to be used in blast furnaces and in making coal gas for illumination. After that, however, the modern era is noted for the rapid appearance of new sources of energy.

Coal ended the long dominance of fuel wood in 1885. As westward expansion occurred, and railroads were built across the country, the demand for coal increased. It remained the principal energy source until 1951, when petroleum, and then natural gas, became the most used energy source.

Petroleum got its initial start as an illuminant and ingredient in patent medicines but did not catch on as a fuel source right away. Petroleum gained increasing importance with the discovery of Texas's vast Spindletop Oil Field in 1901 and with the advent of mass-produced automobiles—several million of which had been built by 1918. World War II also pushed the popularity of petroleum up because trucks ran on gasoline and diesel fuel.

Hydroelectric power appeared in 1890, and nuclear electric power appeared in 1957. Solar photovoltaic, advanced solar thermal, and geothermal technologies represent even more recent developments in energy resource evolution.

The most drastic change to society from energy was largely due to Edwin Drake's introduction of petroleum as an energy source. Although the consumption of petroleum did not take off initially, it climbed drastically in the mid-twentieth century. Neither before nor since has any source of energy become so dominant so quickly.

The first half of the twentieth century in the United States marked the shift from muscle power to machine power. Horses, mules, and other draft animals were invaluable up until the mid-1900s. In 1870, draft animals accounted for more than half of the source of power for transportation and machinery. Their displacement by fossil fuel engines meant the disappearance from cities and farms of millions of animals.

As fossil fuels gained a foothold in the economy, the very nature of work evolved along with the fundamental social and political circumstances in the nation. In the middle of the nineteenth century, most Americans lived in the countryside and worked on farms. By the middle of the twentieth century, the United States had become the world's largest producer and consumer of fossil fuels. Most Americans were city-dwellers, and fewer Americans worked in agriculture. The United States had tripled its per-capita consumption of energy and had become a global superpower.

Most of the energy produced today in the United States—as in the rest of the industrialized world—comes from fossil fuels: coal, natural gas, crude oil, and natural gas plant liquids. Fossil fuels together far exceed all other sources of energy.

Throughout its history, the United States has been mostly self-sufficient in energy production, although small amounts of coal were imported from Britain in colonial times. Through the late 1950s, production and consumption of energy were nearly in balance. Over the following decade, however, consumption began to grow more than domestic production. By the early 1970s, the gap grew even wider—the United States couldn't produce enough energy to meet the demand. According to the U.S. Department of Energy, in 2000 the United States produced just less than 72 quadrillion Btus of energy and exported 4 quadrillion Btus. The American public, however, consumed 98 quadrillion Btus, requiring 29 quadrillion Btus to be imported—this was 19 times the 1949 level of consumption.

Petroleum demand and consumption is the reason the United States must import so much energy. In 1973, the United States imported 6.3 million barrels per day. In October 1973, the Arab members of the Organization of Petroleum Exporting Countries (OPEC) embargoed the sale of oil to the United States, after which prices rose sharply, and petroleum imports fell for two years. Imports increased again until the price of crude oil rose dramatically (1979–1981) and imports lessened. The rising import trend resumed by 1986 and, except for slight dips in 1990, 1991, and 1995, has continued ever since. In 2000, U.S. petroleum imports reached an annual record level of 11 million barrels a day.

Conservation and efficiency have become a trend in the recent past and the efficiency with which Americans use energy has improved over the years. Even though efficiency has increased, however, energy use has historically continued to rise.

Energy plays a crucial role in the operation of the industrialized U.S. economy, and a lot of energy is used. According to the U.S. Department of Energy, American consumers spend more than half a trillion dollars a year on energy. Energy is categorized into four principal uses: residential, commercial, industrial, and transportation. Over the years, industry has used the most energy.

Energy sources have also changed over the years. In the commercial and residential sectors, coal was the leading source of energy until 1951, but then its use declined rapidly. Petroleum usage grew slowly to its peak in 1972 and then subsided. Natural gas became an important resource, growing strongly until 1972, when its growth drastically slowed. The use of electricity, only an incidental source of energy in 1949, has

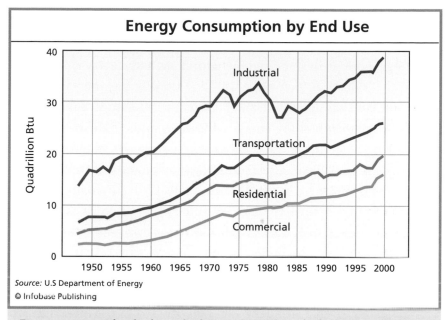

Energy Consumption by End Use

Source: U.S Department of Energy
© Infobase Publishing

Energy consumption in the United States by end use is depicted in the above graph.

expanded in almost every year since then and so have the energy losses associated with producing and distributing the electricity.

According to the U.S. Department of Energy, the drastic increase in electricity has happened mainly in the residential sector—reflecting the increased availability, use, and dependence households have on electrical appliances and systems. For example, in 1997, 99% of U.S. households had a color television set and 47% had central air conditioning. Eighty-five percent of all households had one refrigerator; the other 15% had two or more. In 1978, only 8% of U.S. households had a microwave oven, but by 1997, microwaves existed in 83% of the homes. In 1990, 16% of households owned a personal computer; by 1997, the ownership rate had risen to 35%.

Heating homes in the United States has also involved major shifts in energy sources. For example, in 1950, one-third of the homes were heated by coal; but by 1999, that number had dropped to less than one percent. In 2000, the main sources of energy to heat homes shifted to natural gas and electricity. Like residential buildings, most commercial buildings today are also heated by natural gas and electricity.

In the industrial sector, the use of electricity has increased, while the use of coal has decreased, and petroleum and natural gas have fluctuated. More than half the energy consumed in the industrial sector is used for manufacturing, especially in the petroleum, chemical, metal, and paper product industries. Natural gas is the most commonly consumed energy resource in manufacturing. A relatively small amount of energy is used for other types of manufacturing, such as asphalt roof products, roadbed materials, pharmaceuticals, inks, and adhesives.

Petroleum is the principal source of energy for transportation. Of every 10 barrels of petroleum consumed in the United States in 2000, nearly half were used to make motor gasoline. The five leading suppliers of petroleum to the United States are Saudi Arabia, Canada, Venezuela, Mexico, and Nigeria (Source: U.S. Department of Energy, Energy Information Administration).

Electricity has become an increasingly significant energy resource in the United States. Most electricity is produced from coal (which provides more than half of the electricity generated), hydroelectric power, natural gas and petroleum, and nuclear power.

Just as electricity's applications and sources have changed over time, the structure of the electric power sector is also evolving. It is moving away from the traditional, highly regulated organizations known for decades as electric utilities toward an environment marked by lighter regulation and greater competition from non-utility power producers. Based on data from the U.S. Department of Energy, in 2000, non-utility power producers produced 26% of the total electricity made available.

Modern renewable sources (such as wind, water, and wood) in the United States contribute about as much to total energy consumption, as does nuclear power. Hydroelectric power generation, which uses the water stored in reservoirs behind dams to drive **turbine** generators, accounts for a large share of U.S. renewable energy output.

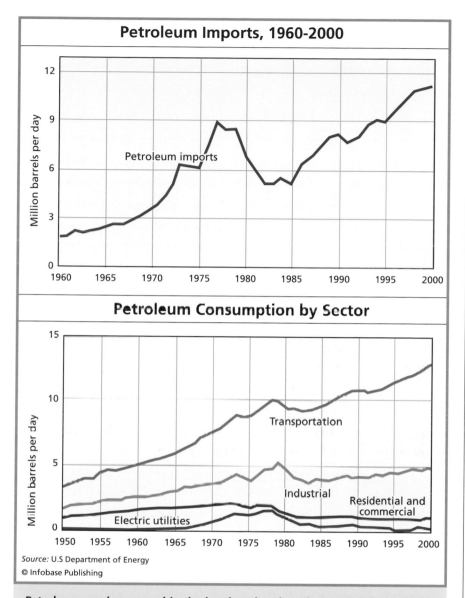

Petroleum Imports, 1960-2000

Million barrels per day

Petroleum imports

Petroleum Consumption by Sector

Million barrels per day

Transportation

Industrial

Residential and commercial

Electric utilities

Source: U.S Department of Energy

© Infobase Publishing

Petroleum use has soared in the last few decades. The top graph shows the increase in petroleum imports by the United States from 1960–2000. The bottom graph indicates the amount of petroleum used by different sectors. The increased consumption of petroleum over the years is primarily due to an increased demand for gasoline and diesel fuel.

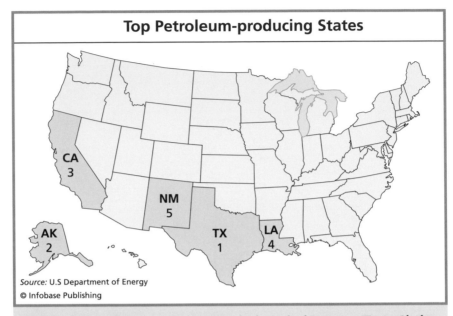

Top Petroleum-producing States

CA
3

NM
5

AK
2

TX
1

LA
4

Source: U.S Department of Energy
© Infobase Publishing

The top five petroleum-producing states in the United States are Texas, Alaska, California, Louisiana, and New Mexico.

Much of U.S. renewable energy today comes from wood and waste. These energy sources include: wood, methanol, ethanol, **peat**, wood liquors, wood sludge, railroad ties, pitch, **municipal solid waste**, agricultural waste, straw, tines, landfill gas, and fish oil. Wood and its by-products are the most heavily used form of biomass and are an important source of energy for such industries as lumber and paper manufacturing. Geothermal energy accounted for 5% of the U.S. renewable energy in 2000.

Solar energy (photovoltaic and thermal) and wind energy contribute least of all to the renewable energy sector—only about 2% in 2000. Most of the solar thermal collectors (91%) went for residential uses, and most of these were used to heat swimming pools. Four percent were used to heat water. Wind energy production rose 113% between 1989 and 2000, but it is still a small component of renewable energy use in the United States.

RENEWABLE AND NONRENEWABLE RESOURCES

There are two general classes of resources: renewable and non-renewable. A renewable resource is a resource that can be replenished. It is a resource that can be replaced by natural ecological cycles, Earth system cycles, and good management practices. The opposite of this is a nonrenewable resource—a resource that cannot be replenished (once it is gone, it is gone for good). For practical applications, scientists consider a renewable resource one that can be replenished within one generation of a human's lifetime (approximately 20–30 years). Resources such as fossil fuels and nuclear energy (uranium) are nonrenewable. Even though the same geologic processes that form them are still happening on the Earth today, these resources will not be replaced within our lifetime because they take millions of years to form. As a result, they are not renewable resources for the present life on Earth.

Even though there are many different types of energy resources, they fit into either a nonrenewable or renewable category. Nonrenewable resources are the fossil fuels and uranium (for nuclear energy). They are the resources being depleted because of constant use. On the other hand, there is no shortage of renewable energy from the sun, wind, and water. Even what is usually thought of as garbage—dead trees, branches, lawn clippings, sawdust, livestock manure, and leftover crops (called biomass)—can produce electricity.

NONRENEWABLE ENERGY RESOURCES

Nonrenewable energy sources come out of the ground as liquids, gases, and solids. Crude oil (petroleum) is the only naturally liquid commercial fossil fuel. Natural gas and propane are normally gases, and coal is a solid stored in beds.

The United States currently gets 88% of its energy from fossil fuel energy sources (Source: U.S. Department of Energy, Energy Information Administration). Fossil fuels—primarily coal, oil, and natural gas—were formed hundreds of millions of years ago, before the time of the dinosaurs, from decomposed plant and animal matter. When fossil fuels are burned, they release greenhouse gases and other pollutants into the **atmosphere**.

Uranium ore, a solid, is mined and converted to a fuel. Uranium is not a fossil fuel—it is a radioactive, metallic element. Nuclear energy, also a nonrenewable resource, provides about 8% of the energy in the United States. Its **radioactive** fuel—typically uranium—is used up in the process of energy production, and the spent radioactive waste must then be stored for tens of thousands of years before it becomes safe. Because of this, there is a high amount of controversy over the use of nuclear power.

Oil (Petroleum)

Oil was formed from the remains of animals and plants that lived millions of years ago in a marine (wet) environment. Over the years, layers of mud covered the remains. Heat and pressure from these layers helped the remains turn into what is referred to as "crude" oil. The word *petroleum* means "rock oil" or "oil from the Earth."

Crude oil is a yellow-to-black liquid and is usually found in large underground areas called reservoirs. Scientists and engineers explore a chosen area by studying rock samples from the Earth. Measurements are taken, and if scientists believe it is a formation that contains oil, drilling begins. Above the hole, a triangular structure called a **derrick** is built to house the tools and pipes that go into the well. Once a well is drilled to the correct depth, a steady flow of oil comes to the surface.

Much of the crude oil in the United States comes from California, Texas, and Louisiana—much of it produced offshore. Even though the United States is one of the world's major oil producers, more than 60% of the crude oil and petroleum products used in the United States are imported from other countries.

After crude oil is removed from the ground, it is sent to a **refinery** by pipeline, ship, or barge. At a refinery, different parts of the crude oil are separated into usable petroleum products. Crude oil is measured in barrels. A 42-U.S.-gallon (158 liter) barrel of crude oil provides a little more than 44 gallons (167 liters) of petroleum products. This 2-gallon (9 liter) gain happens when the crude oil is processed. One barrel of

What a Barrel of Gas Represents

In the early 1860s, when oil production began, there was no standard container for oil, so oil and petroleum products were stored and transported in barrels of all different shapes and sizes, such as beer barrels, fish barrels, molasses barrels, and turpentine barrels. By the early 1870s, the 42-gallon (158 liter) barrel had been adopted as the standard for oil trade—2 gallons (9 liters) more than the 40-gallon (149 liter) barrel that had been previously adopted as the standard for oil trade. This extra oil was to allow for **evaporation** and leaking during transport (most barrels were made of wood). Standard Oil began manufacturing 42-gallon (158 liter) barrels, that were blue, to be used for transporting petroleum. The use of a blue barrel—abbreviated *bbl*— guaranteed a buyer that this was a 42-gallon (158 liter) barrel.

crude oil, when refined, produces 19.9 gallons (75.3 liters) of motor gasoline along with other petroleum products. Most of the petroleum products are used to produce energy—to fuel airplanes, cars, and trucks. Other common products are also made from petroleum, such as ink, bubble gum, crayons, deodorant, dishwashing liquid, eyeglasses, ammonia, tires, records, makeup, plastic products, heart valves, and medicine. Products from oil are used every day in many ways.

There are environmental impacts associated with petroleum, however, such as air and water **pollution**. Over the years, as people have become more environmentally aware, new technologies and laws have been put in place to reduce the negative impacts. Because petroleum has an impact on the environment, the federal government monitors its production, refinement, transportation, and storage. Since 1990, fuels made from petroleum have been improved so that they produce lower amounts of pollution.

Because exploring and drilling for oil can also adversely impact land and ocean habitats, new technology has been developed in recent years to reduce the disturbance. The use of space satellites, global positioning systems, remote sensing (aerial photos and satellite images), and 3-D and 4-D seismic technologies allow engineers and scientists to discover and explore new wells without harming the surrounding natural environment. Due to the invention of movable drilling rigs and smaller drilling rigs, today's production impact is only about one-fourth of what it was 30 years ago, according to experts at the U.S. Department of Energy.

When all the oil from a well is gone, the well is plugged below ground. Some offshore rigs are then knocked over and left on the seafloor to become artificial reefs that attract fish and other marine life, such as coral, sponges, and barnacles.

If oil is spilled into rivers or oceans, it can harm wildlife. Leakage from ships has been reduced since the 1990s, when ships were required to have a "double hull" lining to protect against spills. The largest percentage of oil that leaks into water is from natural oil seeps coming from the ocean floor. Fuel can also leak from motor boats and jet skis and enter the water. Oil products used on land (such as used motor oil) can eventually get washed downstream to contaminate rivers and oceans.

Natural Gas

Natural gas is formed the same way as petroleum—from the remains of ancient plants and animals. Over time, pressure and heat from the Earth changed some of this organic material into natural gas—tiny bubbles of odorless gas. The main ingredient in natural gas is methane, a gas composed of one carbon atom and four hydrogen atoms.

Gas escapes from small spaces in the rocks into the air. When people first saw flames emitted from natural gas areas during electrical storms, they experimented with the gas and discovered how natural gas could be used.

Natural gas is found in geologic settings similar to where petroleum occurs. Geologists use seismic surveys to locate likely areas to drill for gas deposits. They commonly use seismic surveys, which use vibrations on the Earth's surface to send out echoes and collect information about the rocks beneath the ground. If a site looks promising, the area is drilled. Many of the nation's drilling rigs are offshore, deep in the ocean. Once gas is found, it flows up through the well to the surface of the ground and then into large pipelines.

Some of the gases produced—besides methane—are butane and propane. Propane can be used to heat homes or cook food on a barbecue grill. Because natural gas is naturally colorless, odorless, and tasteless, mercaptan (a chemical that smells like sulfur) is added to it as a safety precaution in case of a leak (a natural gas leak can be fatal if a person breathes it in).

Other machines, called "digesters," turn organic material—such as food, plants, animal waste, and garbage composed of these materials—into natural gas. Natural gas is also a raw material for many products used every day, such as paint, fertilizer, antifreeze, plastic, dyes, photographic film, medicines, and explosives. Natural gas has thousands of uses. It is used to produce steel, glass, paper, clothing, brick, and electricity. According to the U.S. Department of Energy, more than 61.9 million homes use natural gas to fuel furnaces, water heaters, and clothes dryers.

Natural gas is one of the "cleaner" fossil fuels because it produces fewer pollutants. It also has fewer emissions than coal or oil and does not release ash particles after it is burned.

Coal

Millions of years ago, huge forests covered the Earth's surface. Some of the forests were later covered by water. The plants died and formed a thick layer of vegetative matter. As it hardened, this layer became peat. Through time, layers of soil and **sediment** covered the peat. Buried under heavy layers of sediment, the peat was protected from the air. Over many years, the peat was transformed into coal.

Throughout geologic time, this process happened repeatedly, which formed distinctive beds of coal. Layers of buried coal are also called coal seams or coal veins. Coal seams usually lie parallel to the Earth's surface, which means the oldest coal is buried the deepest—unless geologic processes have disturbed it and tilted it.

Coal that is mined near the surface of the ground is done using a technique called **strip mining**, also called open cast mining. Miners dig the coal from an exposed seam. Deeper seams are mined using underground tunnels.

According to the U.S. Department of Energy, the United States produces more than one-fifth of the world's coal. Coal is used to generate more than half of all electricity produced in the United States. It is also used as an energy source in the steel, cement, and paper industries. Most U.S. coal beds are located near the ground's surface. Modern mining methods allow easy access to these reserves. Coal is used for four main purposes: for the generation of electric power, for industry, for making steel, and as an export commodity.

Power plants burn coal as a fuel in order to produce steam. The steam is necessary to turn turbines, which generate electricity. Electric utility companies use more than 90% of the coal mined in the United

Coal strip mining, oil refinery, and manufacturing. (a) The predominant underground mining method in the United States is the room and pillar method, a term derived from the mining pattern of a series of excavated areas (rooms) and unexcavated areas (pillars) which are left to support the roof. (b) Miners are protected by the Thyssen roof supports. The canopy extensions are hydraulically operated. The shield supports weigh 17.5 tons (15.9 metric tons) and measure 16.5 feet (5 m) in length. (c) Oil refinery in Salt Lake City, Utah. (d) Manufacturing plants require enormous amounts of power, like this metal-producing plant. *(a, b, courtesy of U.S. Department of Energy; c, d, photos by Nature's Images)*

States. Many industries use coal's heat and by-products. Separated ingredients of coal (such as methanol and ethylene) are used in making plastics, tar, synthetic fibers, fertilizers, and medicines. According to the Energy Information Administration of the U.S. Department of Energy, industry uses more than 6% of the coal mined in the United States.

Coal is baked in hot furnaces to make coke, which is used to **smelt** iron ore into the iron needed for making steel. The extremely high temperatures created for the use of coke gives steel the strength and versatility it requires for use in products such as bridges, buildings, and automobiles.

Uranium and Nuclear Energy

The U.S. Department of Energy has determined that nuclear power accounts for about 20% of the total electricity generated in the United States, an amount comparable to all the electricity used in California, Texas, and New York. In 2003, there were 66 nuclear power plants

The Differences Between Peat, Lignite, Bituminous Coal, and Anthracite

As decaying matter becomes coal, it passes through several stages. The first stage is peat, which forms when layers of plant matter harden. At this point, it does not contain much carbon, so it gives off a lot of smoke when it is burned. After burning, it leaves behind large quantities of ash. Huge deposits of peat are referred to as peat bogs. Peat is used in some countries to heat homes. It is also used as a fuel in factories.

Lignite comes from peat deposits that have been confined under pressure. It is not as black or as dense as other coals. It is more loose-grained and has less carbon, so it does not heat as well as other forms of coal. When lignite is buried under deep pressure, it changes into **bituminous coal**—the most common type of coal. It is black, sooty, has a high degree of carbon, and burns well.

The oldest stage of coal is **anthracite**—the hardest of all the coals. It is shiny and clean. It is rich in carbon, burns slowly, leaves no ash behind, gives off a lot of heat, and lasts a long time.

throughout the United States, located mostly on the East Coast and in the Midwest.

A nuclear power plant operates basically the same way as a fossil fuel plant, with one difference: the source of heat. The process that produces the heat in a nuclear plant is the fissioning—or splitting—of uranium atoms. That heat boils water to make the steam that turns the turbine generator, just as in a fossil fuel plant. The part of the plant where the heat is produced is called the reactor **core**.

Atoms are made up of three major particles: **protons**, **neutrons**, and **electrons**. The most common fissionable atom is an isotope (the specific member of the atom's family) of uranium known as Uranium-235 (U-235 or U^{235}), which is the fuel used in most types of **nuclear reactors** today. Although uranium is fairly common—about 100 times more common than silver—U^{235} is relatively rare. Most U.S. uranium is mined in the western United States. Once uranium is mined, the U^{235} must be extracted and processed before it can be used as a fuel. In its final usable state, the nuclear fuel will be in the form of a pellet roughly 1 inch (2.54 centimeters) long, which can generate approximately the same amount of electricity as 1 ton (0.91 metric tons) of coal.

There are different types of nuclear power plants. Two types are used in the United States: boiling-water reactors (BWRs) and pressurized-water reactors (PWRs). In the BWR, the water, heated by the reactor core, turns directly into steam in the reactor vessel and is then used to power the turbine generator. In a PWR, the water passing through the reactor core is kept under pressure so that it does not turn to steam at all—it remains liquid. Steam to drive the turbine is generated in a separate piece of equipment called a steam generator. A steam generator is a giant cylinder with thousands of tubes in it through which the hot, radioactive water can flow. Outside the tubes in the steam generator, nonradioactive water ("clean" water) boils and eventually turns to steam. The clean water may come from one of several sources—oceans, lakes, or rivers. The radioactive water flows back to the reactor core, where it is reheated, only to flow back to the steam

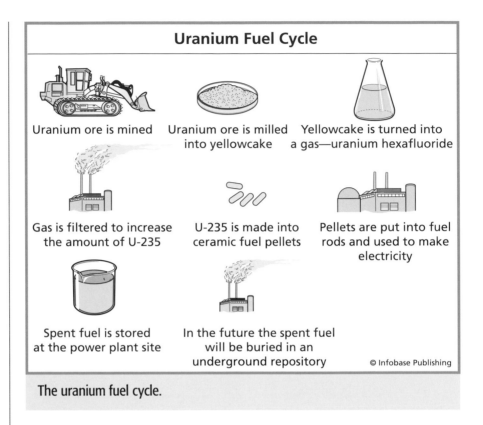

Uranium Fuel Cycle

Uranium ore is mined

Uranium ore is milled into yellowcake

Yellowcake is turned into a gas—uranium hexafluoride

Gas is filtered to increase the amount of U-235

U-235 is made into ceramic fuel pellets

Pellets are put into fuel rods and used to make electricity

Spent fuel is stored at the power plant site

In the future the spent fuel will be buried in an underground repository

© Infobase Publishing

The uranium fuel cycle.

generator. Roughly 70% of the reactors operating in the United States are PWR.

Nuclear reactors are basically machines that contain and control chain reactions, while releasing heat at a controlled rate. In electric power plants, the reactors supply the heat to turn water into steam, which drives the turbine generators. The electricity is shipped or distributed through transmission lines to homes, schools, hospitals, factories, office buildings, rail systems, and other customers.

The reactor core is composed of four main elements: fuel, **control rods**, coolant, and a **moderator**. The nuclear fuel is stored in fuel rods. The fuel consists of pellets of enriched uranium dioxide that are packed into thin metal rods roughly 12 feet (3.7 m) long. Large groups of these rods can be connected in order to allow the power plant to operate for long periods of time.

The control rods are used to regulate (control) the rate of the nuclear chain reaction. For example, if they are pulled out of the core, it speeds up the reaction. Conversely, if they are inserted, the reaction slows down. A coolant—usually water—is pumped through the reactor to carry away the extreme heat generated by fissioning of the fuel in the nuclear reaction. This is comparable to the water in the cooling system of a car, which carries away the heat built up in the engine. A moderator is used to slow down the speed at which energized atoms travel. Water is commonly used for this purpose. This is important because reducing the speed enables atoms to be more likely to split. This splitting is what releases the energy.

Although it may seem like a highly efficient and clean method of producing energy, nuclear power generation does have by-product wastes associated with it in the forms of radioactive waste and hot water. On the positive side, based on studies conducted by the U.S. Department of Energy, because nuclear-generated electricity does not emit **carbon dioxide** into the atmosphere, nuclear power plants in the United States prevent about as much greenhouse emissions as taking 5 billion cars off the streets and highways. Radioactive wastes are the principal environmental concern about using nuclear power. Most nuclear waste is low-level nuclear waste: ordinary trash, tools, protective clothing, wiping cloths, and disposable items that have been contaminated with small amounts of radioactive dust or particles. These materials are subject to special regulations that govern their storage so they will not come in contact with the outside environment.

The irradiated fuel assemblies are highly radioactive and must be stored in specially designed pools resembling large swimming pools (water cools the fuel and acts as a radiation shield) or in specially designed dry storage containers. The older and less radioactive fuel is kept in a dry storage facility, which consists of special concrete-reinforced containers. The U.S. Department of Energy's long-range plan is for this spent fuel to be stored deep in the Earth in a geologic repository, at Yucca Mountain, Nevada. Currently, all spent (used) fuel is stored at the power plant at which it was used.

Oil Shale, Tar Sands, and Natural Bitumen

Oil shales are natural rock formations that contain deposits of kerogen (a type of organic matter), which can be converted into a product resembling petroleum. The term *oil shale* is somewhat misleading, however, because sometimes the rock layer in which the kerogen is trapped is not actual shale, but a rock called *marl*. Natural oil is formed through physical processes that generate great amounts of heat within the Earth's crust. Because oil shale is not subject to these physical processes naturally, it must be artificially heated to a high temperature in order to transform it into a liquid. Scientists believe the oil product produced from oil shale has a quality somewhere between natural oil's low- and high-grade distinctions. Many of the richest oil shale deposits in the world occur in the western United States, in states such as Utah.

There are two ways of processing oil shale. In one method, the rock is fractured in place and heated to obtain the gases and liquids by wells. The second way is by mining, transporting, and heating the shale to about 232°F (450°C), adding hydrogen to the resulting product, and disposing of the waste. Both of these processes use an excessive amount of water. To date, the financial and environmental costs—costs of blasting, transporting, crushing, heating, and adding hydrogen, as well as the safe disposal of huge quantities of waste material—are great enough that large-scale production has not occurred yet in the United States. Oil shale has been used as a low-grade fuel in Estonia and other countries by burning it directly. Unfortunately, this produces a fuel that is high in ash content and harmful to the environment.

Worldwide, use of this fuel is still very limited. According to the U.S. Department of Energy, however, with the current prices of petroleum continuing to rise, oil shale production may be looked at closer as a way to offset the daily consumption of 73 million barrels of oil worldwide. Currently, however, on a small scale, oil shale may be able to make a contribution to the world's energy needs, but so far it is not a viable choice of energy.

Tar sands are sands infused with a heavy oil that require further processing to refine into petroleum products. Some deposits are so heavy that they can be mined more easily than pumped. Tar sands are a mixture consisting of a host sedimentary porous rock of mineral material (usually sand, sandstone, limestone, carbonate rock, or diatomaceous earth), which contains a form of heavy asphalt-like crude oil that is too viscous (thick) to flow through rocks, well bores, or pipelines or to recover by conventional pumping methods.

Although most tar sand deposits are mined, they can also be pumped after high-pressure steam is injected underground to separate the valuable oil from the sand. Hydrogen is added later to turn it into a synthetic crude oil. Producing oil from tar sands is energy intensive, however. The equivalent of one barrel of oil is needed to process three barrels of synthetic crude oil. Production of conventional oil still requires much less energy. Besides being energy intensive, another drawback is that a large amount of waste sand is generated. Using tar sand also contributes to the greenhouse gases in the atmosphere.

The American Association of Petroleum Geologists has determined that tar sands are currently found in about 70 countries around the world. The world's largest deposits are in Canada and Venezuela, and may prove to be critical over the next 50 years to the supply of liquid fuels as the world's production of traditional oil lessens. It will not ultimately solve the need for petroleum, but it may—in the future—provide an avenue to develop new technologies and cleaner fuels.

According to journalist Thomas J. Quinn of the *Cleveland Plain Dealer,* some energy analysts believe emergency programs need to be put in place in order to experiment with, and learn to use, tar sands as an energy source. They believe the peak of oil production will happen sometime between now and the year 2030. Some experts believe Canada may have close to 180 billion barrels of tar sand—roughly a six-year world supply at today's energy consumption rates.

Tar sand production is around 1 million barrels a day and is projected to be five times as much by the year 2030—which is only half of Saudi Arabia's current output of petroleum and less than 5% of world production predicted for 2030. Supporters of tar sand development admit that the technology to use it must be further developed for it to have a significant impact on worldwide energy use.

Natural bitumen and extra-heavy oil are two types of petroleum. Because the lighter elements comprising petroleum are not found in these deposits, they have a higher percentage of heavy **molecules**, making them more dense and viscous (thick).

Natural bitumen and extra-heavy oil occur worldwide. According to the World Energy Council in 2005, the largest bitumen deposit is located in Alberta, Canada, and accounts for about 85% of the world total. Energy experts believe that it may be the only deposit in the world large enough to recover and convert to oil economically. The extra-heavy crude oil deposit of the Orinoco Oil Belt in Eastern Venezuela represents nearly 90% of the known extra-heavy oil in place.

Natural bitumen is also contained in bituminous sands, oil shale, and tar sands. In order to recover it, the petroleum is obtained either as raw bitumen in place or as a synthetic crude oil processed through refinement. So far, these resources have not been explored fully or had their extraction and processing developed in order to be economical. As future energy demands rise and oil becomes scarcer, these forms of energy will become more important to develop.

RENEWABLE ENERGY

Renewable resources offer an immense potential supply of energy. According to the government of California, that state has enough energy in wind gusts to produce 11% of the world's wind electricity. The sunlight that falls on the United States in one day contains more than twice the energy the United States consumes in a whole year. Renewable energy resources are also referred to as "clean" energy. These sources can be harnessed to produce electricity, heat, fuel, and chemicals that are much more environmentally friendly.

As a comparison, emissions from cars that burn gasoline and emissions from industrial factories that use fossil fuels contribute greatly to the **greenhouse effect**. Experts at the U.S. Environmental Protection

Agency believe that about 80% of all the greenhouse gases in the United States are the result of these energy-related sources.

Using renewable energy not only helps the environment, but it helps the economy. Developing and using renewable sources keeps more money at home to bolster the economy of the United States. Also, the more nonrenewable sources that are provided locally, the less energy (fossil fuels) that must be imported from foreign countries. In addition, in this time of such political instability with many of the oil-producing countries in the Middle East, having to import less oil relieves some of the international political tension that currently exists.

Another positive trend with renewable energy resources is that with continued research, development, and experimentation, these sources are becoming more affordable. There are also drawbacks, however. For example, solar energy requires large available areas of land, which can impact wildlife habitat, disturb land use, and degrade the land through construction of roads and buildings. Also, the photovoltaic cells are manufactured using toxic chemicals. In addition, the United States does not currently have enough solar production facilities to meet the current energy demand.

Wind power also requires the use of large areas of land, can cause erosion, can impact wildlife habitat by being a constant danger to birds, and can also degrade the natural view. Geothermal energy is restrictive because geothermal sites only occur in a limited number of places. In addition, the steam can be caustic and corrode the pipes used in energy production.

Hydroelectric power has its drawbacks, too. It causes certain areas of land to become permanently submerged, can impact wildlife habitat, and can cover archaeological sites—a repeated issue in the American Southwest. Downstream, dams can change the chemical, physical, and biological characteristics of the river and land. Although these renewable sources have some drawbacks—generally, usage of large areas of land that affect animal habitats and outdoor scenery—they have much less impact on the environment than nonrenewable sources.

Solar Energy

The Sun has produced energy for billions of years. Solar energy can be converted directly or indirectly into other forms of energy, such as heat and electricity. The major drawbacks of solar energy include the following: (1) the intermittent and variable manner in which it arrives at the Earth's surface and (2) the large area required to collect it at a useful rate.

Solar energy is used for heating water for domestic use, space heating buildings, drying agricultural products, and generating electrical energy. Electric utilities are trying photovoltaic technology, a process by which solar energy is converted directly to electricity. Electricity can be produced directly from solar energy using photovoltaic devices or indirectly from steam generators using solar thermal collectors to heat a working fluid. **Photovoltaic energy** is the conversion of sunlight into electricity. This is accomplished with a device called a photovoltaic (PV) cell—also referred to as a **solar cell**. A PV cell is composed of silicon alloys. When **photons** (particles of solar energy) strike a PV cell, different responses can occur—they may either be reflected, pass through, or become absorbed by the surface. The photons that are absorbed are the critical ones in the photovoltaic process, because the absorbed photons provide the necessary energy to generate electricity. When enough photons are absorbed, the electrons of the surface material of the cell are separated from the atoms. Because of the way the PV cells are produced, more electrons are attracted to the front surface in order to generate energy.

Electrons carry a negative charge. Therefore, when they migrate to the front surface of the PV cell, it causes an imbalance in the distribution of the charge, which in turn creates a **voltage** (the potential energy that pushes a current around an electric circuit).

Because each individual cell only produces a small amount of electricity (1 to 2 watts), PV systems must be made of multiple joined individual cells. When large groups of individual PV cells are connected in formations called modules or arrays, the combined voltage creates usable electricity. An array refers to the entire generating plant, which can be made up from one to several thousand modules.

The amount of electricity produced from a photovoltaic array depends on the amount of available sunlight (it is the photons from the sunlight that enable the creation of electricity). For example, if the skies are overcast, the amount of sunlight is reduced, causing less photons to reach the array, which in turn lowers the amount of electricity the PV array can create. Conversely, clear skies ensure a constant source of sunlight, enabling the array to be highly productive. With today's technology, photovoltaic modules are about 10% efficient in converting available sunlight into energy. Scientists believe that further research on PV arrays will increase their efficiency.

PV cells have had many uses over the years in scientific applications. For instance, in the late 1950s, they were used to provide the power to operate U.S. space satellites. Based on their successful use in space, scientists were then able to use this information to create several commercial applications on Earth. PV cells are commonly used today in calculators and wristwatches, as well as to provide electricity to homes and to power equipment.

The appeal of photovoltaic energy lies in the fact that because the conversion from sunlight to electricity is direct, it eliminates the need to use bulky mechanical generators. They are also portable, easy to assemble, and adjustable, which allows arrays to be installed quickly and in the required configuration for the specific application.

A photovoltaic system is appealing from an environmental standpoint. The impact of a photovoltaic system on the environment is minimal because it does not produce any harmful by-products, and precious water resources do not have to be used for system cooling (as is the case with some other energy sources). They can also generate the direct current (DC) necessary for the operation of electronic equipment. PV cells have also been used to provide electricity for remote sites where installing traditional electric lines is either not feasible nor economical.

The major applications of solar thermal energy today are for heating swimming pools, heating water for domestic use, and heating the insides of buildings. The solar panels are flat-plate solar-energy collectors installed in a fixed position. The highest efficiency is reached when the collector faces toward the south and is inclined horizontally to the location's latitude plus 15 degrees—an angle that best captures the incoming solar energy for that particular point on Earth. For example, a solar-heated home located at a latitude in the United States of 45 degrees would have their solar panels inclined at 60 degrees for the highest efficiency.

Solar collectors can be nonconcentrating or concentrating. In the nonconcentrating type, the collector area (the area that intercepts the solar radiation) is the same as the absorber area (the area absorbing the radiation). This method is commonly used in space heating. In concentrating collectors, the area intercepting the solar radiation is greater than the absorber area. These collectors are used for applications that require higher energy levels.

Solar space-heating systems can also be classified as passive or active. In a passive heating system, the air is circulated past a solar heat surface and through the building by **convection** without the use of mechanical equipment. In active heating systems, mechanical equipment (such as fans and pumps) are used to circulate the warm air or fluid.

Solar thermal power plants use the Sun's rays to heat a fluid, from which heat-transfer systems are used to produce steam, which is then converted into mechanical energy in a turbine. A generator connected to the turbine produces the electricity. The appeal of solar thermal power plants is that the burning of fossil fuels is not necessary. Therefore, these types of power plants do not pollute the environment. There are three types of solar thermal power systems—the parabolic trough, solar dish, and solar power tower.

A parabolic trough is the most advanced of the concentrator systems and is used in large grid-connected power plants. A solar dish uses concentrating solar collectors, which track the Sun's path in the sky, ensuring the dish is always pointed toward the Sun. A solar power tower generates electricity from sunlight by focusing concentrated solar energy on a centrally located, large, tower-mounted receiver. This system can use hundreds to thousands of flat sun-tracking mirrors called heliostats in an array around the tower to reflect and concentrate the Sun's energy onto the central receiver. Power towers are still under development, however, as scientists experiment with the technology, enabling it to be more economical.

Wind Energy

Wind is air in motion. It is produced by the uneven heating of the Earth's surface by the Sun. Since the Earth's surface is made of various land and water formations, it absorbs the Sun's radiation unevenly. This is what causes the uneven heating to occur. When the Sun is shining during the day, the air over landmasses heats more quickly than the air over water. Because warm air is lighter and subsequently rises, it is replaced by the cooler and heavier air that was initially over the water's surface. This process of the air moving across the ocean toward land causes the air to circulate. It is this simple process that creates the local wind system of an area. At night, the winds are reversed because the air cools more rapidly over land than over water. Based on the same principle, the large atmospheric winds that circle the Earth are created because the surface air near the equator is warmed more by the Sun than the air over the North and South Poles. This process is constantly occurring. Because of this, wind is considered a renewable energy resource; it will continually be produced as long as the Sun shines on the Earth—the heat from the sun is the engine that drives the global force. Today, wind energy is typically used to generate electricity.

Windmills work because they slow down the speed of the wind. The wind flows over the airfoil-shaped blades, which causes lift—like the effect on airplane wings in flight—and causes them to turn. The blades are connected to a driveshaft that turns an electric generator to produce electricity.

Today's wind machines are much more technologically advanced than the early windmills. They still use blades to collect the wind's kinetic energy, but the blades are made of fiberglass or other high-strength materials. Modern wind machines are still dealing with the problem of what to do when the wind is not blowing. Large turbines are usually connected to the utility power network—so that some other type of generator picks up the load when there is no wind. Small turbines are sometimes connected to diesel/electric generators or sometimes have a battery to store the extra energy they collect when the wind is blowing hard.

Two types of wind machines are commonly used today—the horizontal-axis with blades like airplane propellers and the vertical-axis, which resembles an egg beater. Horizontal-axis wind machines are more common because they use less material per unit of electricity produced. According to the U.S. Department of Energy, about 95% of all wind machines in use today are the horizontal-axis type. These wind machines are huge. A typical horizontal wind machine stands as tall as a 20-story building and has three blades that span 200 feet (61 m) across. The largest wind machines in the world have blades longer than a football field (300 feet or 91.4 m). Wind machines stand tall and wide to capture more wind. Vertical-axis wind machines make up only 5% of the wind machines used today. The typical vertical wind machine stands 100 feet (30 m) tall and 50 feet (15 m) wide.

Each type of wind machine has its advantages and disadvantages. Horizontal-axis machines need a way to keep the **rotor** facing the wind. This is done with a tail on small machines. Large turbines use either a rotor located downwind of the tower to act like a weather vane, or they use a drive motor. Vertical-axis machines can accept wind from any direction.

Both types of turbine rotors are turned by air flowing over their wing-shaped blades. The vertical-axis blades lose energy as they turn out of the wind, while horizontal-axis blades work all the time. At many sites, the wind speed increases higher above the ground, giving an advantage to tall horizontal-axis turbines. The small tower and ground-mounted generators on vertical-axis turbines also make them cheaper and easier to maintain.

It takes more than one wind machine, however, to produce large amounts of usable energy. Commonly, dozens of wind machines exist in a wind farm array. Interestingly, unlike traditional coal-fired power plants, which are owned by public utility companies, many of today's wind farms are owned by private companies. These independent producers then sell the electricity they produce to electric utility companies, which in turn sell it to their customers. Many customers choose to buy this energy (even though it is slightly more expensive) in order to reduce the known negative impacts on the environment from using fossil fuel energy sources.

Wind power plants cannot be placed in just any random, convenient location, however. Their location must be based on specific factors, such as wind availability (how much the wind blows), local weather conditions, proximity to electrical transmission lines, and local zoning codes. Economics must also be considered, because once a plant has been built, there are maintenance costs. In some states, these costs are offset by tax breaks given to power plants that use renewable energy sources. The Public Utility Regulatory Policies Act, or PURPA, also requires utility companies to purchase electricity from independent power producers at rates that are fair and nondiscriminatory.

Location is one of the most important factors in developing wind farms. Areas where the wind is strong and continuous are the most desirable. The United States has several areas where these conditions apply, such as California, Alaska, Hawaii, the Great Plains, and mountainous regions. In order to generate efficient electricity from wind energy, the wind must have an average speed of 14 mph (22.5 km/h).

There are two different ways to measure the energy the wind provides: efficiency and capacity. *Efficiency* refers to how much useful energy (such as electricity) can be generated from an energy source. A 100% energy-efficient machine would change all the energy put into it into useful energy. It would not waste any energy. There is no such thing as a 100% energy-efficient machine, however. Some energy is always lost or wasted when one form of energy is converted to another. The lost energy is usually in the form of heat, which dissipates into the air and cannot be used again economically. In terms of efficiency, however, wind machines are just as efficient as most other traditional energy plants, such as coal plants. According to the U.S. Department of Energy, wind machines convert 30%–40% of the wind's kinetic energy into electricity. A coal-fired power plant converts about 30%–35% of the chemical energy in coal into usable electricity.

Capacity refers to the capability of a power plant to produce electricity. A power plant with a 100% capacity rating would run all day, every day, at full power. There would be no downtime for repairs or refueling. These types of power plants do not exist. Coal plants typically have a 75% capacity rating since they can run day or night, during any season of the year.

Wind power plants are different from power plants that burn fuel. Wind plants depend on the availability of wind, as well as the speed of the wind. Therefore, wind machines cannot operate 24 hours a day, 365 days a year. A wind turbine at a typical wind plant operates 65%–80% of the time, but usually at less than full capacity, because the wind speed is not at optimum levels or it is sporadic. Therefore, its capacity factor is 30%–35%. Economics also plays a large part in the capacity of wind machines. Wind machines that have much higher capacity factors can be built, but it is not economical to do so—yet.

Based on studies conducted by the U.S. Department of Energy, one wind machine can produce 1.5 to 4.0 million kilowatt-hours (kWh) of electricity each year. That is enough electricity for 150–400 homes. In the U.S., wind machines currently produce 10 billion kWh of energy a year. While this may seem like a lot, wind energy only provides about 0.1% of the nation's electricity—a very small amount. That is enough electricity to serve a million households (an area roughly comparable to a city nearly the size of San Diego, California, or Dallas, Texas). California produces more electricity from the wind than any other state, followed by Texas, Minnesota, and Iowa. California alone has approximately 13,000 wind machines that produce more than 1% of the State's electricity. They expect that within the next 15 years, wind energy may be able to generate 5% of the needed electricity. The reason

California is currently in the lead in wind technology innovation and implementation is due to the positive initiatives that California's state government has taken to support renewable energy in an effort to protect the environment.

There are other states that have wind resources comparable to California's. In fact, ten years ago, the United States was the world's leading producer of wind energy—producing 90% of the world's wind-blown electricity. By 1996, however, that number had dropped to 30%. Wind is the fastest-growing energy technology in the world today. Experts expect the production from wind machines to triple in the next few years. Other areas of the world, including India and many European countries, are planning future wind facilities. Unfortunately, in the United States, wind capacity grew very slowly in the 1990s. Many new wind projects were put on hold because of electricity deregulation. Because utility providers were not sure how deregulation would affect many new technologies, it caused wind technology to come to a temporary standstill. Fortunately, recent investment in wind energy is beginning to increase because its cost has come down and the technology has improved, making wind one of the most competitive new sources for energy generation.

Another positive sign for the wind industry is the growing consumer demand for "green" pricing. Many utilities around the country now allow customers to voluntarily choose to pay more for electricity generated by renewable sources as an effort to protect the environment. Energy experts believe wind energy will become more in demand in the future.

In the 1970s, oil shortages spurred the development of **alternative energy** sources. In the 1990s, renewed interest came from a concern for the environment in response to scientific studies indicating potential changes to the global climate if the use of fossil fuels continues to increase. This situation, termed *global warming,* has gained the attention of many Americans recently and increased the desire to develop economical alternative energy sources. Wind energy offers a viable, economical alternative to conventional power plants in many areas of

Renewable energy sources: (a) Wind turbines at Tehachapi Pass, California. This wind farm, with 5,000 wind turbines, is the second largest collection of wind generators in the world. The turbines produce enough electricity to meet the needs of 350,000 people every year. (b) Vertical axis wind turbines located in Altamont Pass in California. (c) Offshore wind turbine and photovoltaic system, which powers a U.S. Navy offshore test facility. (d) Geysers are natural fountains of hot water found in geothermal areas. (e) This solar energy-collecting unit is located at the California State Polytechnic University. *(a, b, c, e, courtesy of U.S. Department of Energy; d, courtesy of U.S. National Renewable Energy Laboratory, photo by George Kourkouliotis)*

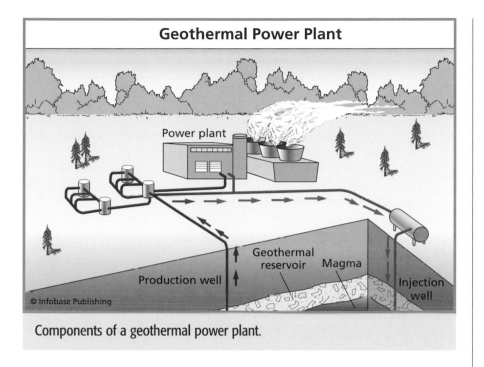

Geothermal Power Plant

Components of a geothermal power plant.

the country. Wind is a clean fuel—wind power plants produce no air or water pollution because no fuel is burned. Also, the cost of producing electricity from the wind has dropped dramatically in the last 20 years. Electricity generated by wind cost 30 cents per kWh in 1975, but now costs less than five cents per kWh. New turbines are lowering the cost even more. The most serious environmental drawbacks to wind machines may be their negative effect on wild bird populations and the visual impact on the landscape.

Geothermal Energy

Volcanic energy cannot be harnessed (controlled and collected), but in a few places, heat from the Earth—called geothermal energy—can be collected. Usually, engineers try to collect this heat in the rare places where the Earth's crust has trapped steam and hot water. At these locations, they drill into the crust and allow the heat to escape, either as steam or as very hot water. Pipes carry the hot water to a plant, where some of the steam is allowed to "flash," or separate from the water. That steam then turns a turbine generator to make electricity.

Geothermal energy was first used to produce electricity in Italy in 1903. At the end of 2002, there were 43 power plants producing electricity from geothermal energy in the United States at facilities located in California, Nevada, Utah, and Hawaii. Generation from geothermal sources is "site specific," meaning it is only possible in a few places under unique geologic conditions. One such site in California, called The Geysers, is able produce almost as much electricity as all the other geothermal sites combined.

Geothermal energy can be used as an efficient heat source in small end-use applications such as greenhouses, but the consumers have to be located close to the source of heat. The capital of Iceland—Reykjavik—is a unique location because it is heated mostly by geothermal energy.

Geothermal energy has a major environmental benefit because it offsets air pollution that would have been produced if fossil fuels had been used instead. Geothermal energy has a very minor impact on the soil—the few acres used look like a small light-industry building complex. Since the slightly cooler water is reinjected into the ground, there is only a minor impact, except if there is a natural **geyser** field close by. For this reason, tapping into the geothermal resources of Yellowstone National Park is prohibited by law.

Biomass—Renewable Energy From Plants and Animals

Biomass is organic material made from plants and animals. Biomass contains stored energy from the sun. Plants absorb the sun's energy in a process called **photosynthesis**. The chemical energy in plants gets passed in the food chain on to the animals and people that eat them. Biomass is a renewable energy source because it is possible to grow more trees and crops. Some examples of biomass fuels are wood, crops, manure, and some garbage.

When burned, the chemical energy in biomass is released as heat. An example of this is wood burning in a fireplace. Wood waste or garbage can be burned to produce steam for making electricity or to provide heat to industries and homes.

Burning biomass is not the only way to release its energy. Biomass can be converted to other usable forms of energy like methane gas or transportation fuels like ethanol and biodiesel. Methane gas is the main ingredient of natural gas. Rotting garbage, agricultural waste, and human waste, release methane gas—also called "landfill gas" or "biogas." Crops like corn and sugarcane can be fermented to produce the transportation fuel ethanol. Biodiesel, another transportation fuel, can be produced from leftover food products like vegetable oils and animal **fats**.

According to the U.S. Department of Energy, biomass fuels provide about 3% of the energy used in the United States, as efforts are underway to develop ways to burn more biomass and less fossil fuels. Using biomass for energy can cut back on waste and support agricultural products grown in the United States. Biomass fuels also have a number of environmental benefits.

The most common form of biomass is wood. For thousands of years, people have burned wood for heating and cooking. Wood was the main source of energy in the United States and the rest of the world until the mid-1800s. In the United States, wood and its waste products (bark, sawdust, wood chips, and wood scrap) provide only about 2% of the energy used today. Biomass continues to be a major source of energy in much of the developing world.

According to data from the U.S. Department of Energy, only 20% of the wood burned in the United States is used for heating and cooking; the rest is used by industries in the manufacture of several commodities, such as paper products and construction materials, as well as to produce the electricity needed in the manufacturing process. Such use by industry presents an efficient way for industries to recycle the waste byproducts generated from the wood they use into energy.

Another source of biomass is garbage—also called municipal solid waste (MSW). Trash that comes from plant or animal products is biomass. Food scraps, lawn clippings, and leaves are all examples of biomass trash. Materials that are made out of glass, plastic, and metals are not biomass because they are made out of nonrenewable materials. MSW can be a source of energy by either burning MSW in waste-to-energy plants or by capturing biogas. In waste-to-energy plants, trash is burned to produce steam that can be used either to heat buildings or to generate electricity. In landfills, biomass rots and releases methane gas, also called biogas, or landfill gas. Some landfills have a system that collects the methane gas so that it can be used as a fuel source. Some dairy farmers collect biogas in tanks called digesters, where they put all the mulch and manure from their barns.

Biofuels are transportation fuels like ethanol and biodiesel that are made from biomass materials. These fuels are usually blended with the petroleum fuels—gasoline and diesel—but they can also be used on their own. The advantage to combining ethanol or biodiesel with fossil fuel is that less fossil fuels are burned resulting in less of an impact on global warming. Ethanol and biodiesel are usually more expensive than the fossil fuels that they replace, but they are also cleaner burning fuels, producing fewer air pollutants.

Ethanol is an alcohol fuel made from the sugars found in grains, such as corn, sorghum, and wheat, as well as potato skins, rice, sugarcane, sugar beets, and yard clippings. Scientists are working on cheaper ways to make ethanol by using all parts of plants and trees. Farmers are experimenting with "woody crops"—mostly small poplar trees and switchgrass—to see if they can be grown efficiently. Most of the ethanol used in the United States today is distilled from corn. About 90% of the ethanol produced in the United States is used to make "E10" or "gasohol," a mixture of 10% ethanol and 90% gasoline. Any gasoline-powered engine can use E10, but only specially made vehicles can run on E85, a fuel that is 85% ethanol and 15% gasoline.

Biodiesel is a fuel made with vegetable oils, fats, or greases—such as recycled restaurant grease. These fuels can be used in diesel engines. Biodiesels are the fastest growing alternative fuel in the United States today. Being a renewable fuel, biodiesel is safe, biodegradable, and reduces the emissions of most air pollutants. Burning biomass fuels does not produce pollutants like sulfur, which can cause **acid rain**. When burned, biomass does release carbon dioxide—a greenhouse gas. But when biomass crops are grown, a nearly equivalent amount of carbon dioxide is captured through the process of photosynthesis. Each of the different forms and uses of biomass impact the environment in a different way.

Because the smoke from burning wood contains pollutants like **carbon monoxide** and particulate matter, some areas of the country will not allow the use of wood-burning fireplaces or stoves on high pollution days. A special clean-burning technology can be added to wood-burning fireplaces and stoves so that they can be used even on days with the worst pollution.

Burning municipal solid waste (MSW or garbage) and wood waste to produce energy means that less of it has to be buried in landfills. Plants that burn waste to make electricity must use technology to prevent harmful gases and particles from coming out of their smokestacks. The particles that are filtered out are added to the ash that is removed from the bottom of the furnace. Because the ash may contain harmful chemicals and metals, it must be disposed of carefully. Sometimes the ash can be used for roadwork or building purposes.

Collecting and using landfill waste and biogas fuel also reduces the amount of methane that is released into the air. Methane is one of the greenhouse gases associated with **global climate change**. Many landfills find it cheaper to just burn off the gas that they collect, however, because the gas needs to be processed before it can be put into natural gas pipelines.

Since the early 1990s, ethanol has been blended into gasoline to reduce harmful carbon monoxide emissions. Blending ethanol into gasoline also reduces toxic pollutants found in gasoline but causes more "evaporative emissions" to escape. In order to reduce evaporative emissions, the gasoline requires extra processing before it can be blended with ethanol. When burned, ethanol does release carbon dioxide, a greenhouse gas. But growing plants for ethanol may reduce greenhouse gases, since plants use carbon dioxide and produce oxygen as they grow—producing a counter-balance process.

Biodiesel is much less polluting that petroleum diesel. It has lower emissions of carbon dioxide, sulfur oxide, particulates, carbon monoxide, air toxins, and unburned hydrocarbons, although it does have slightly elevated emissions of nitrogen oxide. Biodiesel additives can also help reduce sulfur in diesel fuel.

Ocean Energy

Oceans cover more than 70% of the Earth's surface. As the world's largest solar collectors, oceans generate thermal energy from the Sun. They also produce mechanical energy from the tides and waves. Even though the Sun affects all ocean activity, the gravitational pull of the Moon primarily drives the tides, while the wind powers the ocean waves.

For the past thousand years, scientists and inventors have studied ocean energy as they have watched how the ocean waves impact with coastal areas and observed the rise and fall of ocean tides. As early as the eleventh century, millers in Britain figured out how to use tidal power to grind their grain into flour. Only in the past 100 years, however, have scientists and engineers begun to look at capturing ocean energy to actually produce electricity.

Because ocean energy is abundant and nonpolluting, today's researchers are exploring ways to make ocean energy economically competitive with fossil fuels and nuclear energy. European Union (EU) officials estimate that by 2010, ocean energy sources will generate more than 950 **megawatts** (MW) of electricity—enough to power almost a million homes in the industrialized world.

The tides produce energy. Tides are caused by the gravitational pull of the Moon and Sun and the rotation of the Earth. Near shore, water levels can vary up to 40 feet (12 m). However, few locations have good inlets and a large enough tidal range—about 10 feet (3 m)—to produce energy economically.

The simplest generation system for tidal plants involves a dam, known as a barrage, built across an inlet. Sluice gates on the barrage allow the tidal basin to fill on the incoming high tides and to empty through the turbine system on the outgoing tide, which is also known as the ebb tide. There are also two-way systems that generate electricity on both the incoming and outgoing tides. Tidal barrages can affect navigation and recreation, however. Potentially the largest disadvantage of tidal power is the effect a tidal station can have on plants and animals in the estuaries.

Tidal fences can also harness the energy of tides. A tidal fence has vertical-axis turbines mounted in it. The water is forced through the turbines as it passes through the fence. They can be used in areas such as channels between two landmasses. Tidal fences have less impact on the environment than tidal barrages, but they can still disrupt the movement of large marine animals. They are also cheaper to install than tidal barrages.

Tidal turbines are a new technology that can be used in many tidal areas. They are basically wind turbines that can be located anywhere there is strong enough tidal flow. Because water is about 800 times denser than air, tidal turbines have to be much sturdier than wind turbines. This makes them more expensive to build, but they have the advantage of being able to capture more energy.

There is also a lot of energy in ocean waves. According to the U.S. Department of Energy, the total power of waves breaking around the world's coastlines is estimated at 2–3 million megawatts. The west coasts of the United States and Europe, and the coasts of Japan and New Zealand, are desirable sites for harnessing wave energy.

One way to harness wave energy is to bend the waves into a narrow channel, thereby increasing their power and size. The waves can then be channeled into a catch basin or used directly to spin turbines. There are no big commercial wave energy plants yet, but there are a few small ones. Scientists at the Department of Energy believe that small, onshore sites have the best potential for the immediate future—they could produce enough energy to power local communities.

The energy from the sun heats the surface water of the ocean. In tropical regions, the surface water can be 40 or more degrees warmer than the deep water. This temperature difference can also be used to produce electricity. One system—called the Ocean Thermal Energy

Conversion (OTEC)—must have a temperature difference of at least 77°F (25°C) to operate, which limits its use to tropical regions. (Hawaii is a case in point. They have experimented with OTEC since the 1970s.) There is no large-scale operation of OTEC today, because there are still many challenges to overcome. First, the OTEC systems are not very energy efficient. Pumping water is a significant engineering challenge itself. There must also be a method in place to transport the generated electricity to land. Experts at the U.S. Department of Energy believe it will probably be 10 to 20 years before the technology is available to produce and transmit electricity economically from the OTEC systems.

Other types of research are being done to place solar farms over the ocean. Many experts believe the ideal place for solar farms is near the coasts, because they would be less cumbersome to build and be able to be accessed easier. Currently, solar energy is used on offshore platforms and also to operate remotely located equipment at sea. Solar energy is attractive as a potential energy source because it is renewable, it is free, and it does not pollute the environment.

Wind energy, like solar energy, is already used on land. As mentioned earlier, wind turbines and wind power plants can only be placed in specific areas where the wind constantly blows. Along the coast of much of the United States, conditions are favorable toward the use of wind energy. (There are people, however, who are opposed to putting turbines just offshore, because they believe it will spoil the ocean view.) Currently, there is a plan to build an offshore wind plant off the coast of Cape Cod, Maryland. Wind is a renewable energy source that does not pollute, so many people see it as a good alternative to fossil fuels.

Hydroelectric Power

Of the renewable energy sources that generate electricity, hydropower is the most often used. It accounted for 7% of U.S. generation and 45% of renewable generation in 2003 (according to U.S. Department of Energy studies). Hydropower is one of the oldest sources of energy. For example, as we saw earlier, it was used thousands of years ago to turn paddle wheels, which were used to grind grain. The first industrial use

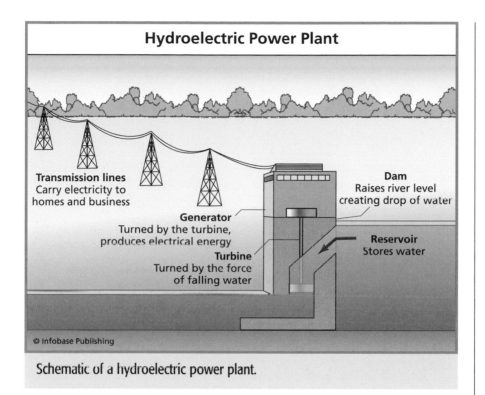

Hydroelectric Power Plant

Transmission lines
Carry electricity to
homes and business

Dam
Raises river level
creating drop of water

Generator
Turned by the turbine,
produces electrical energy

Reservoir
Stores water

Turbine
Turned by the force
of falling water

© Infobase Publishing

Schematic of a hydroelectric power plant.

of hydropower in the United States to generate electricity happened in 1880 in Grand Rapids, Michigan. The first U.S. hydroelectric power plant opened on the Fox River near Appleton, Wisconsin, on September 30, 1882. Up until that time, coal was the only fuel used to produce electricity. Because the source of hydropower is water, hydroelectric power plants must be located on a water source. Therefore, it wasn't until the technology to transmit electricity over long distances via transmission lines was developed that hydropower became widely used.

Directing, harnessing, or channeling moving water drives mechanical energy. The amount of available energy in moving water is determined by the rate at which it flows or falls. Swiftly flowing water in a big river carries a great deal of energy in its flow. Similarly, water descending rapidly from a very high point also carries a great deal of energy as it falls. The water flows through a pipe—also called a penstock—and then pushes against and turns the blades in a turbine to spin a generator in order to produce electricity. In a "run-of-the-river" system, the force of the current applies the needed pressure, while in a storage system, water is accumulated in reservoirs created by dams and then released when the demand for electricity is high. Meanwhile, the reservoirs or lakes are used for boating and fishing, and often the rivers beyond the dams provide opportunities for white-water rafting and kayaking.

The U.S. Department of Energy has determined that 56% of the total U.S. hydroelectric capacity for electricity generation is concentrated in three states: Washington, California, and Oregon. Only a small percentage of all dams in the United States produce electricity. Most other U.S. dams were constructed mainly to provide irrigation and flood control.

Hydropower is an ideal fuel for electricity generation because, unlike the nonrenewable fuels used to generate electricity, it is almost free, there are no waste products, and it does not pollute the water or the air. It is sometimes criticized, however, because it does change the environment by affecting natural habitats. For example, in the Columbia River in Washington, salmon must swim upstream to their spawning grounds to reproduce, but the series of dams gets in their way. Different approaches to fixing this problem have been used, including the construction of "fish ladders" that help the salmon "step up" the dam to the spawning grounds upstream.

As the world's energy demand increases, fossil fuels become less accessible, and people learn more about the benefits to health and life of maintaining a clean environment, the renewable resources covered in this chapter will become increasingly important.

DEVELOPMENT OF ENERGY RESOURCES

This chapter focuses on the development of various forms of energy and the sometimes complicated processes they must go through to reach the consumer. It begins by looking at electricity—where it comes from, how it works, and the roles of magnets, batteries, generators, turbines, transformers, and power plants. Next, it looks at the development of nuclear energy and how it is used to protect the welfare of a country. The chapter then focuses on the trans-Alaska oil pipeline, what the pipeline means to the supply of energy, and the truly remarkable engineering technology behind its creation. Next, the chapter examines the development of the biomass program and hydrogen energy. It concludes with the development of fuel cells and what that means for the future.

THE DEVELOPMENT OF ELECTRICITY

Although electrical power arrived only a hundred years ago, it has completely transformed and expanded humans' energy use. Before electricity generation began, houses were lit with kerosene lamps, food was cooled in iceboxes, and wood- or coal-burning stoves warmed buildings. The development of electricity was a great step forward because it eliminated the need to use sources of energy that were "dirty" fuels, such as wood, coal, and whale oil. Electricity, at the point of use, is clean, flexible, controllable, safe, effortless, and instantly available. Electricity continually improves peoples' lives at home, work, school, and enables entertainment. It runs everything from vacuum cleaners to televisions, microwaves, and DVDs to heating and indoor lighting systems. Electricity outside powers traffic lights, lights up buildings, and helps operate some mass transit systems, such as light rail trains. It enables global communication and powers everything from businesses and manufacturing plants to the computers that run the Internet. In fact, the standard of living enjoyed in the United States today would not be possible without it.

The development of electricity happened over time. Humphrey Davy built a battery-powered arc lamp in 1808, and Michael Faraday an induction dynamo in 1831; but it was another half-century before Thomas Edison's primitive cotton-thread filament burned long enough to prove that a workable electric light could be made. After Edison's discovery, progress accelerated. The first electricity-generating plant was opened three years later in London in January 1882, followed by the first American plant in New York later that September.

BASIC CONCEPTS OF ELECTRICITY

Electricity is the flow of electrical power or charge. It is considered a secondary energy source, which means it is created from the conversion of other sources of energy, such as coal, oil, natural gas, nuclear power, or hydropower—all of which are referred to as primary energy sources. The energy source that is used to make electricity can be renewable or nonrenewable, but electricity itself is neither renewable nor nonrenewable.

Electricity is a basic part of nature and is one of the most widely used forms of energy. In order to understand electricity, it is important to understand the concept of atoms. Everything in the universe is made of atoms—every star, every tree, every animal, every plant, the water, and the air. The human body is made of atoms. Atoms are the building blocks of literally everything; and they are so small that millions of them can fit on the head of a pin.

Atoms consist of three components. The center of an atom is called the nucleus. The nucleus is made of particles called protons and neutrons. The protons and neutrons are very small, but electrons are even smaller. Electrons spin around the nucleus a great distance from the nucleus. Therefore, atoms are mostly empty space.

The electrons orbit in circular paths, called "shells," around the nucleus. They are constantly spinning and moving to stay as far away from each other as possible. Electrons are held in their shells by an electrical force.

The protons and electrons are attracted to each other. They both carry an electrical charge. The electrical charge is a force within the particle. Protons have a positive charge (+) and electrons have a negative charge (−). The positive charge of the protons is equal to the negative charge of the electrons. Opposite charges attract each other. When an atom is in balance, it has an equal number of protons and electrons. The neutrons carry no charge and their numbers can vary.

The number of protons in an atom determines what kind of atom, or element, it is. Electrons usually remain a constant distance from the nucleus in precise shells. The shell closest to the nucleus can hold two electrons. The next shell outward can hold up to eight. The outer shells can hold even more. Some atoms have as many as seven shells of electrons around them.

The electrons in the shells closest to the nucleus have a strong force of attraction to the protons. Sometimes the electrons in the outermost shells do not. These electrons can be pushed out of their orbits. Applying a force can make them move from one atom to another. An atom that loses electrons has more protons than electrons and becomes positively charged. An atom that gains electrons has more negative particles and is negatively charged. A "charged" atom is called an ion. These moving electrons are electricity.

Electricity is always moving in the world. Lightning is one example of electricity. It is created from the electrons moving from one cloud to another or jumping from a cloud to the ground.

Magnets

In most objects, all of the forces are in balance. Half of the electrons are spinning in one direction; half are spinning in the other. These spinning electrons are scattered evenly throughout the object.

Magnets are different. In magnets, most of the electrons at one end are spinning in one direction, while most of the electrons at the other end are spinning in the opposite direction. This creates an imbalance in the forces between the ends of a magnet, and creates a **magnetic field** around the magnet. A magnet is labeled with north (N) and south (S) poles. The magnetic force in a magnet flows from the north pole to the south pole.

When two north poles are put together, they repel (push away from) each other because like forces do not attract each other; but when a north and south pole are put together, they come together with a strong force. Just like protons and electrons, opposites attract. These special properties of magnets can be used to generate electricity. Moving magnetic fields can pull and push electrons. Magnets and wire are used together in electric generators.

Batteries

A battery produces electricity by using two different metals in a chemical solution. A chemical reaction between the metals and the chemicals frees more electrons in one metal than in the other. One end of the battery is attached to one of the metals; the other end is attached to the other metal. The end that frees more electrons develops a positive charge and the other end develops a negative charge.

If a wire is attached from one end of the battery to the other, electrons flow through the wire to balance the electrical charge. A load is a device that performs a job. If a load—such as a lightbulb—is placed along the wire, the electricity can do work as it flows through the wire.

Although energy cannot be created or destroyed, it can be saved in various forms, for example, in a battery. This is referred to as stored energy. When connected in a circuit, a battery can produce electricity.

Inside the battery, a reaction between the chemicals takes place. But reaction only takes place if there is a flow of electrons. Batteries can be stored for a long time and still work because the chemical process does not start until the electrons flow from the negative to the positive terminals through a circuit.

Circuits

Electricity travels in closed loops, or circuits. It must have a complete path before the electrons can move. If a circuit is open, electrons cannot flow. When the circuit is closed—such as flipping a light switch—electricity flows from the electric wire through the light and back into the wire. When the light switch is flipped off, the circuit is opened, and no electricity flows to the light.

When a light switch is turned on, electricity flows through a tiny wire in the bulb. The wire gets very hot and makes the gas in the bulb glow. When the bulb burns out, the tiny wire is broken, and the path through the bulb is gone. Similarly, when a TV is turned on, electricity flows through wires inside the set, producing pictures and sound.

Generators

An electric generator is a device for converting mechanical energy into electrical energy. This process is based on the relationship between magnetism and electricity. When a wire or other conductive material moves across a magnetic field, an electric current occurs in the wire.

The large generators used by the electric utility industry have a stationary (located in one place) conductor. A magnet attached to the end of a rotating shaft is positioned inside a stationary conducting ring that is wrapped with a long, continuous piece of wire. When the magnet rotates, it establishes a small electric current in each section of wire as it passes. Each section of wire constitutes a small separate electric conductor. All the small currents of individual sections add up to one current of considerable size, which is what is used for electric power.

Turbines

An electric utility power station uses a turbine, engine, water wheel, or other similar machine to drive an electric generator or a device that converts mechanical or chemical energy to generate electricity. Steam turbines, internal-combustion engines, gas combustion turbines, water turbines, and wind turbines are the most common methods to generate electricity. Most power plants are about 35% efficient. That means that for every 100 units of energy that go into a plant, only 35 units are converted to usable electrical energy.

Most of the electricity in the United States is produced in steam turbines. A turbine converts the kinetic energy of a moving fluid (liquid or gas) to mechanical energy. Steam turbines have a series of blades mounted on a shaft against which steam is forced, thereby rotating the shaft connected to the generator. In a fossil-fueled steam turbine, the fuel is burned in a furnace to heat water in a boiler to produce steam.

Coal, petroleum (oil), and natural gas are burned in large furnaces to heat water to make steam that in turn pushes on the blades of a turbine. More than half of the United States' electricity uses coal as its source of energy.

Natural gas, in addition to being burned to heat water for steam, can also be burned to produce hot combustion gases that pass directly through a turbine, spinning the blades of the turbine to generate electricity. Gas turbines are commonly used when electricity utility usage is in high demand. According to the U.S. Department of Energy, 16% of the nation's electricity is fueled by natural gas.

Petroleum can also be used to make steam to turn a turbine. Residual fuel oil, a product refined from crude oil, is often the petroleum product used in electric plants that use petroleum to make steam. Petroleum is used to generate about 3% of all electricity generated in the United States.

Nuclear power is a method in which steam is produced by heating water through a process called nuclear fission. In a nuclear power plant, a reactor contains a core of nuclear fuel, made primarily of enriched uranium. When atoms of uranium fuel are hit by neutrons

(a) Electric power is generated from generating stations. (b) Transmission lines carry the electricity to users. *(Photos by Nature's Images)*

that fission (split), they release heat and more neutrons. Under controlled conditions, these other neutrons can strike more uranium atoms, splitting more atoms, and so on. Thereby, continuous fission can take place, forming a chain reaction releasing heat. The heat is used to turn water into steam, which, in turn, spins a turbine that generates electricity. Nuclear power is used to generate 20% of all the United States' electricity.

Hydropower, the source for almost 7% of U.S. electricity generation, is a process in which flowing water is used to spin a turbine connected to a generator. There are two basic types of hydroelectric systems that produce electricity. In the first system, flowing water accumulates in reservoirs created by the use of dams. The water falls through a pipe called a penstock and applies pressure against the turbine blades to drive the generator to produce electricity. In the second system, called "run-of-river," the force of the river current (rather than falling water) applies pressure to the turbine blades to produce electricity.

Geothermal power comes from heat energy buried beneath the surface of the earth. In some areas of the country, enough heat rises close to the surface of the Earth to heat underground water into steam, which can then be tapped for use at steam-turbine plants. This energy source typically generates less than 1% of the electricity used in the United States.

Wind power is derived from the conversion of the energy contained in wind into electricity. Wind power, which is less than 1% of the nation's electricity, is a rapidly growing source of electricity. A wind turbine is similar to a typical windmill.

Solar power is derived from the energy of the Sun. However, solar power is not constant. The Sun's energy is not available full-time and it is widely scattered. The processes used to produce electricity using the Sun's energy have historically been more expensive than using conventional fossil fuels. Photovoltaic conversion generates electric power directly from the light of the Sun in a photovoltaic (solar) cell. Solar-thermal electric generators use the radiant energy from the Sun to produce steam to drive turbines. Less than 1% of the nation's electricity is based on solar power.

Biomass includes wood, municipal soil waste (garbage), and agricultural waste, such as husks and wheat straw. These are some of the other energy sources for producing electricity. These sources replace fossil fuels in the boiler. The combustion of wood and waste creates steam that is typically used in conventional steam-electric plants. Biomass accounts for about 2% of the electricity generated in the United States.

Transformers

To solve the problem of sending electricity over long distances, George Westinghouse developed a device called a transformer that allowed electricity to be efficiently transmitted over long distances. This development made it possible to supply electricity to homes and businesses located away from the electric generating plant.

The electricity produced by a generator travels along cables to a transformer, which changes electricity from low voltage to high voltage. Electricity can be moved long distances more efficiently by using high voltage. Transmission lines are used to carry the electricity to a substation. The long, thick cables of transmission lines are made of copper or aluminum, because they have a low resistance to electricity. Substations have transformers that change the high voltage electricity into lower voltage electricity. From the substation, distribution lines carry the electricity to homes, offices, factories, and other buildings that require low voltage electricity.

Rather than traditional overhead lines, some new distribution lines are now buried underground. The advantage in this is that these power lines are protected from the weather, preventing them from being broken during a storm. Most power lines, however, are still above ground and are vulnerable to damage during extreme weather events.

When electricity enters homes and other buildings, it must pass through a meter. A utility company employee reads the meter so the company will know how much electricity has been used. After being metered, the electricity goes through a fuse box and into the building. The fuse box is a safety precaution designed to protect the building. When a fuse (also called a circuit breaker) "blows" or "trips," something is wrong with an appliance or something has short-circuited.

NUCLEAR ENERGY DEVELOPMENT

From the early 1900s, scientists have known that electrons are held in the atom by electromagnetism, but the forces that hold the nucleus together are much greater. These forces are the key to nuclear power. There are two main ways by which they can release energy: fission and fusion.

In nuclear fission, when a neutron hits an unstable nucleus, the nucleus is split into two smaller, more stable nuclei. Two or three neutrons are usually released as a result of the collision. These neutrons can cause other nuclei to break up, and can cause a chain reaction. The "spare" energy released is in the form of heat.

In nuclear fusion at very high temperatures, small nuclei can be fused together to make larger ones. If the new nucleus needs less energy to hold it together than the old one, energy will be released. The most common fusion reaction is the one that builds a nucleus of helium from nuclei of hydrogen. This reaction has been carried out in special fusion reactors, and many researchers hope that it will be the energy source of the future. It would be clean, safe, and there would be no radioactive waste.

In each case, a reaction occurs in the nuclei of the atoms, and the matter left after the reaction has a little less mass than before. The "lost" mass is changed into energy, some of which is released as high-energy electromagnetic radiation. The rest becomes heat, which can be used to destroy things (by nuclear weapons), or to generate electricity (in nuclear reactors). Atomic bombs are a result of nuclear fission.

Nuclear power stations also use fission. These stations have a reactor core, a heat exchanger, and turbines. The core is where the nuclear reactions take place. In a reactor core, nuclear reactions are carefully controlled by the insertion of materials called "moderators," which absorb free neutrons so they do not increase the rate of the chain reaction. The heat exchanger takes heat from the core to a supply of water. The water is converted into high-pressure steam, and the steam drives the turbine generator to produce electricity.

The atomic age—one of history's most important developments—took centuries to arrive, with accomplishments and discoveries being made by scientists in many countries worldwide. (It was an early Greek thinker named Democritus that first proposed the atomic theory. He believed that everything in the universe was made up of particles so tiny that nothing smaller could exist.)

Nuclear energy has played a critical role in military applications—especially in World War II. In 1939, people believed the Nazis were developing an atomic bomb, which prompted the U.S. Army Corp of Engineers to begin its own bomb development program in June of 1942. The United States wanted to build an atomic weapon before Germany and Japan did.

Albert Einstein wrote a letter to President Franklin D. Roosevelt, convincing him it was important that the United States develop an atomic bomb before anyone else. President Roosevelt's response ultimately led to the Manhattan Project. Experiments to develop the

Nuclear Energy Facts

- As of June 2005, 31 countries worldwide were operating 440 nuclear plants for electricity generation. Twenty-four new nuclear plants were under construction in eight countries.
- Nuclear energy has been used since 1953 to power U.S. Navy vessels and since 1955 to provide electricity for home use.
- The average electricity production cost in 2004 for nuclear energy was $1.68 per kilowatt-hour. For coal-fired plants it was $1.90, for oil it was $5.39, and for gas it was $5.87.
- The energy in one uranium fuel pellet—the size of the tip of your little finger—is the equivalent of 17,000 cubic feet (480 cubic meters) of natural gas, 1,780 pounds (807 kilograms) of coal, or 149 gallons (564 liters) of oil.
- The largest man-made source of radiation is medical diagnosis and treatment, including X-rays, nuclear medicine, and cancer treatment.
- One radioactive isotope, called molybdenum-99, is used about 40,000 times a day in the United States to diagnose cancer and other illnesses.
- Radiation is used to sterilize baby powder, bandages, contact lens solution, cosmetics, and food.

Source: Nuclear Energy Institute

bomb began beneath the University of Chicago's abandoned Stagg Field, where scientists learned more about atomic theory. The first controlled nuclear reaction took place under Stagg Field.

In order to obtain fuel for the atomic bomb, a lab in Oak Ridge, Tennessee, separated the nuclear fuel U^{235} from natural uranium U^{238}. At the same time, scientists at Hanford, Washington, worked on producing plutonium.

General Leslie R. Groves, Deputy Chief of Construction of the U.S. Army Corp of Engineers, was appointed to direct this top-secret project. Many top scientists and engineers worked in Los Alamos, New Mexico, in order to create the first atomic bomb. Once uranium fission was discovered in 1938, the race between countries to be the first to develop the atomic bomb had begun.

In 1942, at the University of Chicago, Enrico Fermi oversaw the first controlled energy release from the nucleus of the atom. Bomb grade U^{235} was produced and shipped to Los Alamos. By 1945, the U.S. had successfully created an atomic bomb. In March of that year, the bomb code named Little Boy was dropped on Hiroshima, Japan.

Many political experts believe that the outcome of World War II hinged on the successful development of the atomic bomb. Since then, many believe that nuclear weapons have helped to keep peace by acting as a deterrent to war.

Nuclear energy is also an important and viable source of power. President Dwight Eisenhower first proposed that the United Nations oversee nuclear energy's international role in sustainable energy development. In his "Atoms for Peace" address to the United Nations in 1953, he recommended that the United Nations form an international nuclear energy organization to make available the humanitarian benefits of nuclear energy worldwide.

The United Nations' International Atomic Energy Agency began operation in 1957. Since then, it has assisted in international development and expansion of nuclear technology for energy, agriculture, medicine, food preservation, hydrology, industry, and ecology.

Many environmentalists believe that of all energy sources, nuclear energy has the lowest impact on the environment because nuclear

The devastation of nuclear weapons. (a) A mushroom-shaped cloud is generated by a U.S. military weapons test in 1952. (b) Smoke billows 20,000 feet (6,100 m) above Hiroshima, Japan, after the detonation of the first atomic bomb used in warfare. *(a, photo courtesy of National Nuclear Security Administration/Nevada Site Office; b, courtesy of U.S. Air Force)*

power plants do not emit harmful gases and require a relatively small area to operate in. As an energy source, it produces the most electricity in relation to its minimal environmental impact.

It is an emission-free energy source because it does not burn anything to produce electricity. Nuclear power plants produce no gases such as nitrogen oxide or **sulfur dioxide** that could threaten the atmosphere by causing ground-level ozone formation, smog, and acid rain. Nor does nuclear energy produce carbon dioxide or other greenhouse gases that cause global warming.

Water discharged from a nuclear power plant contains no harmful pollutants and meets the regulatory standards for the temperatures required to protect aquatic life. This water, used for cooling, never comes in contact with radioactive materials. If the water from the plant is so warm that it may harm marine life, it is cooled before it is discharged to its source river, lake, or bay as it is either mixed with water in a cooling pond or pumped through a **cooling tower**.

The areas around nuclear power plants are often developed as wetlands that provide nesting areas for waterfowl and other birds, new habitats for fish, and the preservation of other wildlife. Many energy companies have created special nature parks or wildlife sanctuaries on plant sites.

Because nuclear power plants produce a large amount of electricity in a relatively small space, they require significantly less land for their operation than all other energy sources. For example, solar and wind farms must occupy substantially more land, and must be sited in geographically unpopulated areas far from energy demand. According to the Nuclear Energy Institute, to build the equivalent of a 1,000-megawatt nuclear plant, a solar park would have to be larger than 35,000 acres, and a wind farm would have to be 150,000 acres or larger.

Some endangered species—such as osprey, peregrine falcons, bald eagles, and red-cockaded woodpeckers—have found a home at nuclear power plants. The plants also provide habitat for species that are not endangered, such as bluebirds, wood ducks, kestrels, sea lions, wild turkeys, and pheasants.

Other people, however, who oppose the development and use of nuclear energy believe that the radioactive material from a nuclear power plant could harm life in the areas surrounding them if there were to be a leak. The threat of terrorist attacks also makes many people nervous to live near a nuclear power plant, in case the plant is attacked, causing a radiation leak. The issue of nuclear energy development has remained a heated debate for decades.

THE TRANS-ALASKA PIPELINE

The construction of the trans-Alaska pipeline is one of the most remarkable feats of engineering ever undertaken. It is one of the largest pipeline systems in the world. Completed in 1977, the trans-Alaska pipeline covers 800 miles (1,276 km) of mountain, muskeg, and river valleys in its span from Prudhoe Bay on Alaska's north slope, to Valdez, the northernmost ice-free port in North America. This is roughly the distance from Los Angeles to Denver.

The pipe is a tube of ½-inch-thick (5 cm) steel with a diameter of 48 inches (122 cm), wrapped with four inches (10 cm) of fiberglass **insulation**. The closer oil is to the molten core of the Earth, the hotter it is when it reaches the surface. Oil pumped from the Prudhoe Bay field, which is 10,000–20,000 feet (3,048–6,096 m) deep, is about 145–180°F (293–356°C). Using heat exchangers that work like a car's radiator, the oil companies cool the oil to about 120°F (248°C) before they pump it into the pipeline.

Engineers would have buried the entire pipeline had it not been for permafrost—the permanently frozen soil that lies in sheets and wedges beneath the ground's surface. The pipeline couldn't be buried in permafrost because the heat of the oil would cause the icy soil to melt. The pipe would then sag and possibly leak. Because permafrost underlies much of Alaska, over half the pipeline is maintained above ground.

Where it snakes over the land, posts designed to keep permafrost frozen support the pipeline. Topped with fanlike aluminum radiators, the posts absorb cold from the winter air and transfer it to the soil. When the air temperature is –40°F (–40°C), for example, the posts cool down to that temperature and take away heat from the soil, assuring the ground stays frozen.

The pipeline was built in a zigzag pattern to allow the pipe to expand and contract. Because workers welded much of the pipeline at temperatures well below zero, engineers anticipated that the metal would expand once hot oil began flowing through. The zigzag also allows the pipeline to flex during earthquakes—it slides over H-shaped supports with the aid of Teflon-coated "shoes" that stand on the crossbar between the posts holding up the pipeline. Where the pipeline crosses seismic faults—weak areas of rock that rupture during earthquakes—it sits on rails that allow it to move side to side should an earthquake cause the Earth's crust to slip sideways along a fault line.

The temperature within the pipeline is relatively constant despite ambient temperatures along the line that can range from nearly 100°F (38°C) to –80°F (–62°C). The four inches (10 cm) of fiberglass

The trans-Alaska pipeline. The pipeline extends more than 800 miles (1,290 km) and represents a remarkable engineering achievement. *(Photo by Patrick J. Endres, AlaskaPhotoGraphics.com)*

insulation that surround the aboveground pipeline keep the oil warm enough to flow even on the coldest winter days. If the pipeline had to be shut down in the winter, the oil within it could sit for several months before congealing.

Powered by 10 pump stations along its length, oil flows through the pipeline at about the speed of the Yukon River—roughly 5–7 mph (8–11 km/h). At that rate, it takes about five-and-a-half days for the oil to complete its journey from Prudhoe Bay to Valdez. Since its construction, the pipeline has successfully transported over 14 billion barrels of oil. It is an important component for supplying energy to consumers.

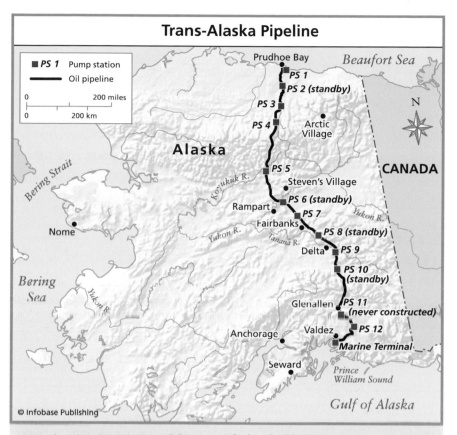

Trans-Alaska Pipeline

■ *PS 1* Pump station
—— Oil pipeline

0 _____ 200 miles
0 _____ 200 km

Prudhoe Bay   *Beaufort Sea*

PS 1
PS 2 (standby)
PS 3
PS 4   • Arctic Village

Alaska   N

Bering Strait

PS 5
Steven's Village   **CANADA**

Kojukuk R.
PS 6 (standby)
Rampart   PS 7   *Yukon R.*
Fairbanks
Nome   *Yukon R.*   *Tanana R.*   PS 8 (standby)
Delta • PS 9
PS 10 (standby)

Bering Sea   *Yukon R.*

Glenallen   PS 11 (never constructed)
Anchorage •   Valdez   PS 12
Marine Terminal
Seward   *Prince William Sound*

© Infobase Publishing   *Gulf of Alaska*

Map showing the location of the trans-Alaska pipeline. It travels from Prudhoe Bay on Alaska's North Slope south to Valdez, the northernmost ice-free port in North America.

BIOMASS PROGRAM DEVELOPMENT

Biomass is plant matter such as trees, grasses, agricultural crops, or other biological material. It can be used as a solid fuel, or converted into liquid or gaseous forms, for the production of electric power, heat, chemicals, or fuels. The U.S. government's National Renewable Energy Laboratory (NREL) is currently working to develop cost-effective, environmentally friendly, biomass conversion technologies to reduce the nation's dependence on foreign oil, improve air quality, and support America's rural economies—which are the source of the biomass.

As continued research and development goes into using biomass to produce energy, more and more uses for it are being discovered. The U.S. Department of Energy has been focusing for the past several years on biomass characterization, thermochemical and biochemical biomass conversion technologies, bio-based products development, biomass process engineering and analysis, and biomass in photochemical and environmental applications.

Biorefineries

A biorefinery is a facility that integrates biomass conversion processes and equipment to produce fuels, power, and chemicals from biomass. Similar to a petroleum refinery, a biorefinery can produce multiple fuels and products from petroleum. Industrial biorefineries have been identified by the NREL as the most promising solution to the creation of a new domestic bio-based industry.

A biorefinery that can produce many types of products has the advantage of maximizing the biomass material (called feedstock) and getting the most value and efficiency that is possible from the materials within one facility. For example, a biorefinery can produce one or many low-volume, but high-value, chemical products and a low-value, but high-volume, liquid transportation fuel, while at the same time generating electricity and processing heat for its own use and perhaps enough excess electricity for sale. The advantages of this type of setup are that the high-value products pay for the refinery, the large amounts of fuel help meet national energy needs, and the power production reduces costs and avoids greenhouse gas emissions.

There are two types of platforms used in biorefineries—a "sugar platform" and a "syngas platform." These two platforms produce different products. The sugar platform is based on biochemical conversion processes and focuses on the fermentation of sugars extracted from biomass feedstocks. The syngas platform is based on the thermochemical conversion processes and focuses on the gasification of biomass feed-stocks and by-products from conversion processes.

Bioproducts

The products that can be made from fossil fuels can also be made from biomass. These bioproducts—also called bio-based products—are not only made from renewable sources, they usually require less energy to produce than petroleum-based products.

Researchers have discovered that the process for making biofuels—releasing the sugars that make up starch and cellulose in plants—can also be used to make antifreeze, plastics, artificial sweeteners, glues, and gel for toothpaste.

Other important building blocks for bioproducts include carbon monoxide and hydrogen. When biomass is heated with a small amount of oxygen, these two gases are produced in abundance. Scientists call this mixture biosynthesis gas. It can be used to make plastics and acids, which can be used in making photographic films, textiles, and synthetic fabrics.

When biomass is heated without oxygen, it forms pyrolysis oil. A chemical called phenol can be extracted from pyrolysis oil. Phenol is used to make wood adhesives, molded plastic, and foam insulation.

Biopower

Biopower, or biomass power, is the use of biomass to generate electricity. There are six major types of biopower systems: direct-fired; cofiring; gasification; anaerobic digestion; pyrolysis; and small, modular.

Most of the biopower plants in the world use direct-fired systems. These plants burn bioenergy feedstocks directly to produce steam. A turbine usually captures this steam, and a generator then converts it into electricity. In some industries, the steam from the power plant is also used for manufacturing processes or to heat buildings. These are known as combined heat and power facilities. For example, wood waste is often used to produce both electricity and steam at paper mills.

Many coal-fired power plants can use cofiring systems to significantly reduce emissions, especially sulfur dioxide emissions. Cofiring involves using bioenergy feedstocks as a supplementary energy source in high-efficiency boilers.

Gasification systems use high temperatures and an oxygen-starved environment to convert biomass into a gas that is a mixture of hydrogen, carbon monoxide, and methane. The gas fuels what is called a "gas turbine," which is similar to a jet engine, only it instead turns an electric generator.

The decay of biomass produces methane gas, which can also be used as an energy source. In landfills, wells can be drilled to release the methane from the decaying organic matter. Then pipes from each well carry the gas to a central point where it is filtered and cleaned before burning. Methane can also be produced from biomass through a process called "anaerobic digestion." Anaerobic digestion involves using bacteria to decompose organic matter in the absence of oxygen.

Methane can be used as an energy source in many ways. Most facilities burn it in a boiler to produce steam for electricity generation or for industrial processes. Two new ways of using methane include the use of microturbines and fuel cells. Microturbines have outputs of 25–500 **kilowatts** (**kW**). Roughly the size of a refrigerator, they can be used where there are space limitations for power production. Methane can also be used as the "fuel" in a fuel cell. Fuel cells work much like batteries but never need recharging—they produce electricity as long as there is fuel available.

In addition to gas, liquid fuels can be produced from biomass through a process, discussed earlier, called pyrolysis. Pyrolysis occurs when biomass is heated in the absence of oxygen. The biomass then turns into a liquid called pyrolysis oil, which can be burned like petroleum to generate electricity.

Several biopower technologies can be used in small, modular systems. A small, modular system is defined as one that generates electricity at a capacity of 5 megawatts or less. This system is designed for use at the small town or consumer level. For example, some farmers use the

Biomass development. (a) A technician adjusts a fast-pyrolysis vortex reactor. The reactor produces adhesives while reducing reliance on fossil fuels. (b) Examples of plastic products that can be made from pyrolysis oil. (c) A fermentation tank with pumps and piping. This system converts animal waste into methane gas. (d) Sludge from paper mills is being used to produce levulinic acid. In the future, the acid may be used to make automotive fuel. *(Photos courtesy of NREL)*

waste from their livestock to provide their farms with electricity. Not only do these systems provide renewable energy, they also help farmers and ranchers meet environmental regulations.

Small, modular systems also have potential as distributed energy resources. Distributed energy resources are a variety of small, modular power-generating technologies that can be combined to improve the operation of the electricity delivery system.

Developing and using biomass energy not only helps America's environment and provides income for farmers, it also serves to reduce our dependence on imported oil. According to the U.S. Department of Energy, in 2002, fossil fuels supplied 86% of the energy consumed in the United States. Also, the United States imports more than half (62%)

Renewable Diesel Fuel

Biodiesel

Biodiesel is made by transforming animal fat or vegetable oil with alcohol and can be directly substituted for diesel either as neat fuel (B100) or as an oxygenate additive (usually 20%—called B20). B20 earns credits for alternative fuel use under the Energy Policy Act of 1992, and it is the only fuel that does not require the purchase of a new vehicle. In Europe, which is the largest producer and user of biodiesel, the fuel is usually made from rapeseed (canola) oil. In the United States, the second largest producer and user of biodiesel, the fuel is usually made from soybean oil or recycled restaurant grease. In 2002, 15 million gallons (56.8 million L) of biodiesel was consumed in the United States.

E-diesel

E-diesel is a fuel that uses additives in order to allow blending of ethanol with diesel. This fuel includes ethanol blends of 7%–15% and up to 5% special additives that prevent the ethanol and diesel from separating at very low temperatures or in the event of water of its petroleum. Unfortunately, this dependency on foreign sources is increasing. Since the U.S. economy is so closely tied with petroleum products and oil imports, small changes in oil prices or disruptions in oil supplies can have an enormous impact on the economy—in areas such as trade deficits, industrial investments, and employment levels. The stress of this was felt by both consumers and businesses when oil prices skyrocketed in 2006. Secondary effects impacted industries that rely on petroleum products, such as the travel industry. Many people elected to travel less because the price of gas was too high. As a domestic, renewable energy source, biomass offers an alternative to conventional energy sources and provides national energy security, economic growth, and environmental benefits.

---

contamination. Use of E-diesel would also increase demand for ethanol, as diesel vehicles in the United States consume approximately 36 billion gallons (136 billion L) of diesel a year.

E-diesel is currently an experimental fuel and is being developed by many companies, who can receive a federal ethanol tax credit when blending ethanol with diesel. Demonstrations are currently being conducted on the use of E-diesel in heavy-duty trucks, buses, and farm machinery. There is a slight increase in operating costs due to a slight (7%–10%) mileage decrease with E-diesel use. However, there are many environmental benefits to using E-diesel, such as reduced emissions of particulate matter, carbon monoxide, and nitrogen oxide.

Supporters of E-diesel see it as a major new market for ethanol and an effective way to help engine manufacturers meet tough new emission standards set by the U.S. Environmental Protection Agency. For instance, it can take up to 10 years for manufacturers to phase in new engine designs that reduce emissions and meet the tough new EPA standards; however, switching to E-diesel brings immediate benefits to the environment.

THE DEVELOPMENT OF HYDROGEN ENERGY

Hydrogen is the simplest element known to man: Each atom of hydrogen contains only one proton and one electron. Hydrogen is also the most plentiful gas in the universe. For example, stars are made primarily of hydrogen.

The sun—a star whose energy also comes from hydrogen—is a giant ball of hydrogen and helium gases. Inside the sun, hydrogen atoms combine to form helium atoms. This process—called fusion—gives off radiant energy. This radiant energy sustains life on Earth and it is stored in fossil fuels. Most of the energy we use today initially came from the sun.

Pure hydrogen gas (H_2) is rare on Earth. Instead, it is commonly mixed with other natural elements. For instance, when it is combined with oxygen, it is water (H_2O). When combined with carbon, it makes different compounds such as methane (CH_4), coal, and petroleum. Hydrogen is also found in all growing things. Hydrogen has the highest energy content of any common fuel by weight, but the lowest energy content by volume. In its pure state, it is lighter than any other element.

Most of the energy we use today comes from fossil fuels, but as people become more environmentally responsible, they want to use more renewable energy. It is usually cleaner and can be replenished in a short period of time. Renewable energy sources—like solar and wind—cannot produce energy all the time. As discussed before, the Sun does not always shine and the wind does not always blow. Renewables do not always make energy when or where they are needed. Many energy sources, however, can be used to produce hydrogen. Hydrogen also has the ability to store energy until it is needed.

Many scientists look at hydrogen as an energy carrier for the future because it is a clean fuel that can be used in places where it is hard to use electricity. Based on calculations by the U.S. Department of Energy, sending electricity a long way costs four times as much as shipping hydrogen by pipeline.

Since pure hydrogen is rare on Earth, it must be made by separating it from water, biomass, or natural gas. Scientists have even discovered that some algae and bacteria also give off hydrogen. Although it is not economical to produce hydrogen at the present time, experts believe that eventually technology will create economically feasible ways to produce it in the future.

Hydrogen also has the flexibility to be produced at large central facilities or at small plants for local use. Equally promising, the Department of Energy has determined that every region of the country has some resource that can be used to make hydrogen. Its flexibility is one of its main advantages.

Nine million tons of hydrogen are produced in the United States today—enough to power 20–30 million cars or 5–8 million homes according to the Energy Information Administration Office of the U.S. Department of Energy. Most of this hydrogen is used by industry in refining, treating metals, and processing foods. The National Aeronautics and Space Administration (NASA) is the primary user of hydrogen as an energy carrier; it has used hydrogen for years in the space program. Hydrogen fuel is what lifts the space shuttle into orbit. Hydrogen batteries—called fuel cells—power the shuttle's electrical systems. The only by-product is pure water, which the crew uses as drinking water.

Hydrogen fuel cells (batteries) are used to produce electricity. They are very efficient, but currently expensive to build. Small fuel cells can power objects such as electric cars. Larger fuel cells are able provide greater amounts of electricity in remote areas, thereby increasing the efficiency of the fuel cells. The larger the capacity of the fuel cell, the more power that can be successfully generated.

Because of the cost, hydrogen power plants will not be built in the immediate future. Hydrogen may soon be added to natural gas, though, to reduce pollution from existing plants. Soon hydrogen will be added to gasoline to boost performance and reduce pollution. It has been determined that increasing the hydrogen content of gasoline to 5% can significantly lower emissions of nitrogen oxides, which contribute to ground-level ozone pollution. An engine that burns pure hydrogen produces almost no pollution. According to the U.S. Department of

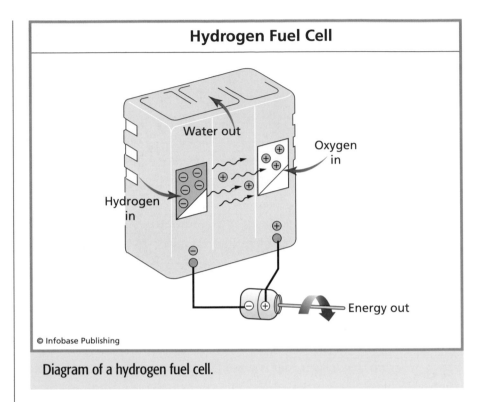

Hydrogen Fuel Cell

Water out

Oxygen in

Hydrogen in

Energy out

© Infobase Publishing

Diagram of a hydrogen fuel cell.

Energy, it will probably be 10–20 years before hydrogen-powered cars become available.

DEVELOPMENT OF FUEL CELLS

A fuel cell is a device that generates electricity by a chemical reaction. Every fuel cell has two electrons—one positive and one negative—called the cathode (which is positive) and anode (which is negative). The reactions that produce electricity take place at the electrodes. Every fuel cell also has an electrolyte, which carries electrically charged particles from one electrode to the other, and a catalyst, which speeds the reactions at the electrodes.

The basic fuel for fuel cells is hydrogen. One of the most attractive benefits of fuel cells are that they generate electricity with very little pollution—much of the hydrogen (H) and oxygen (O) used in generating electricity ultimately combine to form a harmless by-product—water.

A chemist tests a solid-oxide fuel cell. *(Courtesy NREL)*

A single fuel cell generates a tiny amount of direct current (DC) electricity. When fuel cells are used, they are usually assembled into a stack.

The purpose of a fuel cell is to produce an electrical current that can be directed outside the cell to do work, such as powering an electric motor, operating lightbulbs, or supplying electricity. Because of the way electricity behaves, the current that is generated returns to the fuel cell, completing the electrical circuit. The chemical reactions that produce this current are the key to how a fuel cell works. In general terms, hydrogen atoms enter a fuel cell at the anode where a chemical reaction strips them of their electrons. The hydrogen atoms are then *ionized* and carry a positive electrical charge. The negatively charged electrons provide the current through wires to do work. If alternating current (AC) is needed, the DC output of the fuel cell is routed through a conversion device called an inverter.

In some fuel cells, oxygen enters the fuel cell at the cathode and combines with electrons returning from the electrical circuit and hydrogen ions that have traveled through the electrolyte from the anode. In other fuel cells, the oxygen picks up electrons and then travels through the electrolyte to the anode, where it combines with the hydrogen ions. Together, oxygen and hydrogen form water, which drains from the cell. As long as a fuel cell is supplied with hydrogen and oxygen, it will generate electricity.

One of the major advantages of fuel cells is that they create electricity chemically—instead of from combustion—so they are not subject to the thermodynamic laws that control a conventional power plant. Because of this, fuel cells are more efficient. Waste heat from some cells can also be used, making them an even more efficient energy source.

Building inexpensive, efficient, reliable fuel cells is still complicated with today's technology, however. Scientists and inventors have designed many types and sizes of fuel cells. There are several types of electrolytes used, such as alkali, molten carbonate, phosphoric acid, proton exchange membrane, and solid oxide. Some cells need pure hydrogen, requiring them to have a "reformer" to purify the fuel. Others need higher temperatures to be efficient.

Each type of fuel cell has its own advantages and drawbacks, and they are all still very expensive to produce. At this point, their efficiency needs to be further developed and improved in order to compete economically with coal-fired, hydroelectric, or nuclear power plants. Alkali fuel cells have been used by NASA on the space shuttle and the Apollo programs. They are highly efficient—about 70%—and also provide drinking water for the astronauts.

Many companies today are examining ways to reduce the costs and improve the versatility of fuel cells. The transportation industry is interested in using them as an energy source. In 1998, a prototype taxi in London, England, was introduced by the Zero Emission Vehicle Company (ZEVCO). It uses a 5,000-watt alkali fuel cell that does not produce noxious fumes and is much more quiet than normal combustion vehicles. Other vehicles using fuel cslls are also being tested today, such as delivery vans, airport tow-tugs, and power boats. Fuel cells are also being experimented with in submarines, sonobuoys, power plants, and even in homes as a principal source of energy.

CHAPTER 5

THE USES AND IMPACTS OF ENERGY

Just as there are many types of available energy resources found on Earth, there are many uses for these energy resources, as well. The United States is a highly developed and industrialized society. A lot of energy gets used in homes, businesses, industry, and for traveling to and from these places each day. This chapter examines and compares energy uses for residential, commercial, industrial/manufacturing, transportation, and communication applications. It also looks at current uses of alternative energy. Finally, it explores the impacts on the environment of various types of energy use.

RESIDENTIAL ENERGY USE

For thousands of years, people have used energy to cook their food and to provide heat and light in their homes. Energy to accomplish these tasks was usually obtained from fire created by burning wood, oil, or candles. During the nineteenth century, coal gas began to be used in millions of homes in many countries. Later, powerful electrical genera-tors were built to supply electricity to homes.

Uses of Energy in Homes

Based on estimates of the U.S. Department of Energy, the energy used in homes accounts for 20% of all the energy consumed in the United States. The ability to control the indoor temperature is one of the most important achievements of modern technology. To control the tem-perature of the air inside a home, the temperature of an oven or stove, or a refrigerator or freezer is a luxury humans have only had for the past few decades—it was not possible even 100 years ago. Controlling these temperatures, however, takes a lot of energy. Almost half of the average home's energy consumption is used for heating. According to the U.S. Department of Energy, another 17% of energy consumption is used to heat the water, 6% is used to operate air conditioners to cool rooms, and 5% is used to keep refrigerators and freezers cold.

Most homes still use the traditional incandescent lightbulbs invented by Thomas Edison. These bulbs convert only about 10% of the electricity they use to produce light—the other 90% is converted into heat, which is why lightbulbs get so hot. As technology has pro-gressed over the years, however, incandescent bulbs have become more efficient than they used to be due to better gas mixtures and filament designs. In 1879, the average bulb produced only 14 lumens per watt. (A lumen is a measure of light with an intensity equal to one candle.) Today, lightbulbs produce about 17 lumens per watt. When halogen gases are added, the efficiency can be increased to 20 lumens per watt.

Compact fluorescent bulbs (also called CFLs) have become more common in home lighting systems in the past few years. Although these bulbs are more expensive, they last much longer and—more impor-tant—use less energy.

Appliances, such as refrigerators, freezers, washing machines, and dryers are more energy efficient than they used to be. In 1990, Congress passed the National Appliance Energy Conservation Act, which requires all new appliances to meet strict **energy efficiency** standards.

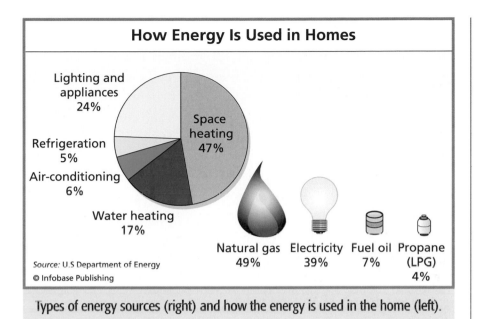

How Energy Is Used in Homes

Lighting and appliances
24%

Refrigeration
5%

Air-conditioning
6%

Space heating
47%

Water heating
17%

Natural gas
49%

Electricity
39%

Fuel oil
7%

Propane (LPG)
4%

Source: U.S Department of Energy
© Infobase Publishing

Types of energy sources (right) and how the energy is used in the home (left).

Types of Energy Used in Homes

Natural gas is the most widely used energy source in American homes, followed by electricity, heating oil, and propane. Natural gas and heating oil (fuel oil) are used mainly for home heating. Electricity may also be used for heating and cooling, plus it lights homes and runs almost all appliances, including refrigerators, freezers, toasters, blenders, vacuums, microwave ovens, and computers. Many homes in rural areas where gas lines have not been installed use propane for heating, while others use it to fuel their barbecue grills.

Energy Used in Different Types of Homes

The U.S. Department of Energy has determined that about 80% of residential energy use is consumed in single-family homes, while 15% is consumed in multifamily dwellings such as apartments, and 5% is consumed in mobile homes.

More than half of the energy used for heating in single-family homes is natural gas, about one-fourth is electricity, and one-tenth is fuel oil (heating oil). Over three-fourths of single-family homes have some type of air-conditioning. Almost all single-family homes have a washing machine and a dryer; and more than half own a personal computer, further emphasizing the importance of energy resources.

Multifamily dwellings, such as apartments and condominiums, use about equal amounts of natural gas and electricity for heating. About two-thirds of multifamily homes have air-conditioning but only about one-fourth contain washers and dryers.

Mobile homes are more likely than the other types of homes to heat with propane (LPG). More than one-third of mobile homes use electricity and about one-third use natural gas for heating. Most mobile homes also contain washing machines and dryers.

COMMERCIAL ENERGY USE

The commercial sector uses about 16% of the nation's energy. The commercial sector includes offices, stores, hospitals, schools, police stations, warehouses, hotels, barbershops, libraries, shopping malls, restaurants, churches, community centers, civic centers, and many other buildings.

Energy Use in Commercial Buildings

Commercial buildings all have unique energy needs, but, as a whole, commercial buildings use more than half their energy for heating and lighting. Electricity and natural gas are the most common energy sources used in commercial buildings. Commercial buildings also use another source that is usually not found in residential buildings—district energy. When there are many buildings close together, such as a college campus, a government complex, or a resort complex, it is sometimes more efficient to have a central heating and cooling plant that distributes steam or hot water to all of the different buildings in the cluster. A district system can reduce equipment and maintenance costs, as well as save energy.

Energy Use by Type of Building

Retail and service buildings use the most total energy of all the commercial building types, partly because of the high numbers of stores and service businesses that exist in most towns. Offices use almost as great a share of energy as retail and service. Educational buildings—such as schools—use 11% of all total energy, which is even more than all hospitals and other medical buildings combined. Warehouses, lodging, and food service (restaurants) each use 8% of all energy. Public assembly buildings, which can be anything from libraries to sports arenas, use 6%; food sales buildings (such as grocery stores and convenience stores) use 4%. All other types of buildings, including churches, fire stations, police stations, and laboratories, account for the remaining 7% of commercial building energy.

INDUSTRIAL AND MANUFACTURING ENERGY USE

The United States is a highly industrialized country. Industry accounts for about one-third of the energy used in the country. There are many different energy uses and a variety of different energy sources in the manufacturing sector. One main use is as boiler fuel to generate steam or hot water. Another use is as process heating, which is when energy is used directly to raise the temperature of products in the manufacturing process, such as when separating components of crude oil in petroleum refining or cooking packaged foods.

Types of Energy for Industry and Manufacturing

In the manufacturing sector, the predominant energy sources are natural gas and electricity (a secondary source). Manufacturers also use other energy sources for heat, power, and electricity generation. They use many uncommon energy sources as a feedstock (a raw material used to make other products).

Every industry uses energy, but there are a handful of energy-intensive industries that use the bulk of the energy consumed by the industrial sector. Petroleum refining is the largest industrial consumer of energy, followed by the chemical industry. The paper and metal industries also use a great deal of energy to produce their products.

TRANSPORTATION ENERGY USE

Moving people and goods from place to place is a vital part of any civilization. The earliest ways of getting around made use of animals and wind as energy sources. Toward the end of the eighteenth century, the first canals were built. Then, at the beginning of the nineteenth century, the steam engine was developed and the first railroads were built. By the end of the nineteenth century, the internal combustion engine had been perfected and cars were invented. As technology improved in the twentieth century, streetcars and aircraft were developed.

The United States relies heavily on transportation. In fact, about 27% of the energy used goes to transporting people and goods from one place to another. Cars, vans, and buses are commonly used to carry people. Trucks, airplanes, and railroads can be used to carry people and freight, while barges and pipelines only carry freight. In 2001, there were almost 217 million vehicles (cars, buses, and trucks) in the United States—roughly three motor vehicles for every four people.

The U.S. Department of Energy determined that cars, motorcycles, trucks, and buses were driven over 2.7 trillion miles in 2001—a distance comparable from the Earth to the Sun and back 13,440 times!

Types of Energy Used for Transportation

Gasoline is used mainly by cars, motorcycles, and light trucks; diesel is used mainly by heavier trucks, buses, and trains. Together, gasoline and diesel make up 85% of all the energy used in transportation. There is currently a push to develop vehicles that run on fuels other than petroleum products, or that run on blended fuels. Today, there are some vehicles that run on electricity, natural gas, propane, and ethanol. Hybrid vehicles use much less gasoline than normal vehicles because they also run on electricity part of the time.

Personal vehicles (such as cars and light trucks) consume almost 60% of the total energy used for transportation, while commercial vehicles (such as large trucks and construction vehicles), mass transit (such as airplanes, trains, and buses), and pipelines account for the rest of the energy used.

Oil goes through a refinery where it is made into many different products. Some of them are used for transportation, such as aviation fuel, gasoline, and diesel fuel. From the refinery and larger storage tank farms, transportation fuels are usually trucked to service stations in tanker trucks.

At service stations, the two grades of gasoline, regular and premium, are kept in separate underground storage tanks, from where they are pumped into cars. Midgrade gasoline is a combination of the two types. Other vehicles, such as trucks and some cars use diesel fuel, which is also made from oil.

Burning gasoline, however, creates air pollution. Because of this, oil companies are creating newer types of gasoline that are cleaner than the kind used today. This newer "reformulated gasoline" will be a better type of fuel for the environment. Fuels are being developed from sources other than oil—such as methanol, ethanol, natural gas, propane, and even electricity. Collectively, they are referred to as alternative fuels because they are an alternative to traditional gasoline

Did You Know?

- The abbreviation *bbl* stands for "blue barrel." Barrels, especially made for transporting oil, were originally painted blue to assure buyers that they were 42-gallon barrels, instead of the 40-gallon barrels used by some other industries.
- When natural gas is burned, it produces mostly carbon dioxide and water vapor—the same substances emitted when people breathe.
- Natural gas is odorless, but has an organic compound called mercaptan added to give it an odor, enabling leaks to be detected.
- If all the passenger vehicles in the United States were lined up bumper to bumper, they would reach all the way from the Earth to the moon and back. The amount of fuel consumed in these vehicles each year is enough to fill a swimming pool as big as a football field that is 40 miles (64.4 km) deep.

Source: U.S. Department of Energy

and diesel. Cars and trucks that use them are called Alternative Fuel Vehicles, or AFVs.

Currently, there are only a small number of cars and trucks running on fuels other than gasoline and diesel, but the trend is on the rise. In the future, experts believe these alternative sources will become much more widespread.

ENERGY FOR COMMUNICATION

All forms of communication require energy to create, send, and receive. Because energy is necessary for communication, transmitting over large distances was difficult before the invention of electricity. Once electricity was developed, communication became much faster.

The first large-scale form of communication to utilize electricity was the telegraph. The first successful telegraph was constructed in 1837. After its creation, many more electrical communication systems were developed over the next century. In the 1880s, the telephone was invented, totally revolutionizing global and local communication.

The first signal using electromagnetic waves was sent in the 1890s. By the early 1900s, radio waves were being used to communicate over large distances. By the 1930s, radio communication had become a daily part of peoples' lives. As computers and satellite technology were developed worldwide, communication became faster, easier, and more efficient. The past few decades have seen an explosion in communication technology using energy. Satellites transmit sound, pictures, and data around the world. Global positioning systems (GPS) are used by pilots, sailors, the military, and search and rescue organizations for precise geographic orientation. They have even advanced to the point that they are affordable for the general public, and are used in many activities such as hiking, recreation, mapping, surveying—even as personal emergency systems with services such as OnStar.

Cell phones also represent a huge technological advancement, as does the speed of computers and the creation of the Internet. All these conveniences that people use today use energy in order to work. The advancements of modern science and energy have changed the lifestyles of almost every person on Earth—the impacts are truly amazing.

ALTERNATIVE ENERGY USE

Alternative energy sources have many uses in society today. Many alternative renewable sources are also referred to as "green energy," signifying environmentally friendly energy sources. Fortunately, over the years, there has been a trend toward conservation and the use of many alternate energy resources. The greater use of conservation-oriented and cost-effective renewable resources is a positive step for the nation as a whole, and many believe the development of clean, renewable energy resources is where research and development efforts should be directed in the future. For example, technology today has enabled different sources of fuel—such as solid waste, landfill gas, wastepaper, biomass, and sugar cane wastes—to be used to provide the energy for power plants in order to produce more energy for consumers.

Methane

A primary constituent of natural gas, methane is an important energy source. Utilizing methane emissions can provide significant energy, economic, and environmental benefits. There are a variety of natural and human-influenced sources of methane: landfills, natural gas and petroleum, agricultural activities, coal mining, wastewater treatment, and certain industrial processes.

A feasible method of methane recovery is anaerobic digestion of livestock waste. When manure is broken down through microbial action, it releases the methane gas as an energy source. It also creates soil-building by-products in the form of liquids and biosolids. Methane gas can be used to produce electricity from local electric power suppliers in rural areas, which in turn supports the economic development in that community.

Recovering methane also helps the environment when it's converted into an energy source. This helps to keep methane out of the atmosphere. Methane is a greenhouse gas that remains in the atmosphere for about 9–15 years. According to the U.S. Department of Energy, methane is more than 20 times more effective in trapping heat in the atmosphere than carbon dioxide is over a 100-year period.

The most feasible methane—also called biogas—sources for conversion to electricity are from large animal enterprises where enough manure is available to make the energy conversion practical. This requires an operation with a minimum of 300 dairy or beef animals, or 2,000 pigs. These animals are usually kept confined so that the manure can be collected regularly.

Electricity generated from "green sources" often attracts a new market that is even willing to pay more for their power in order to promote environmental protection. Besides biogas, other green sources of electricity include ocean energy, wind energy, solar energy, landfill gas, and even the burning of alfalfa stems and other feedstock.

Ocean Energy

Right now, there are very few ocean energy power plants, and most are fairly small. There are three basic ways to tap the ocean for its energy: waves, high and low tides, and temperature differences.

Wave energy can be used to power a turbine. The rising water forces the air out of the chamber, and the moving air spins a turbine that can turn a generator. When the wave goes down, air flows through the turbine and back into the chamber through doors that are normally closed. Another type of wave energy system uses the up-and-down motion of the wave to power a piston that moves up and down inside a cylinder. The piston can also turn a generator, creating power. Most wave-energy systems today are small, and can be used to power a warning buoy or a small lighthouse.

Tidal energy utilizes the tides when they come into shore. Dams can be built across narrow inlets, which allow the water to enter a reservoir. When the reservoir becomes filled, the dam is closed and the water is trapped in the inlet. Then, when the tide goes out hours later and the water level drops on the ocean side of the dam, the water that was retained in the reservoir can be released. The energy of the water rushing out of the reservoir powers the turbines that produce electricity.

There are two types of tidal energy dams. Some are constructed so that electricity can be generated when the tide comes into the reservoir and again when it goes out. Others are constructed so that electricity is produced when the tide leaves the reservoir only. These facilities cannot be built just anywhere, however. They only work in areas that have relatively large changes in the tides. In fact, electricity can be produced only if the difference between low and high tide is at least 16 feet (4.9 m). There are a limited number of areas worldwide that meet these conditions.

Using the temperature differences in ocean water to generate electricity is not a new idea, either. The idea dates from the 1880s, when a French engineer named Jacques D'Arsonval, first developed the concept. Today, power plants can use the difference in ocean water temperatures to make energy. A difference of at least 38°F is needed between the warmer surface water and the colder deep ocean water to make this work. This technology is currently being used in Hawaii to produce electricity.

Wind Energy

As we saw in Chapter 3, wind is another viable energy resource to produce electricity. However, wind power production is very land intensive—it requires large areas of land in order to put up enough wind machines to make it feasible. Wind power requires sustained winds of 14 mph (22.5 km/h) or stronger, making America's deserts and mountain ranges some of the most suitable places for wind energy technology.

Wind power used to provide energy to ships is not new and is still used to propel them. Today, however, it is mainly used for sport and leisure—for yachts, sailboats, sailing dinghies, and sailboards. There is also an interest in using wind power for commercial shipping. A few passenger liners, oil tankers, and other large commercial ships have been equipped with sails. They use their sails when the wind is strong enough, but switch to engine power when the wind speed drops.

Using sail power with an engine as a back-up power source cuts costs and pollution by reducing the amount of fuel that has to be burned. If the wind is strong enough, it can also reduce voyage times. First launched in France in 1990, the Club Med I is an example of a wind-powered luxury ship. One of the world's largest sailing ships, it is a new concept of luxury passenger liner designed to utilize the power of the wind. Not only does it use sails, but its seven sails are all computer controlled. Computers continually monitor the sails and adjust them to receive their best performance.

Solar Sources

Solar power is now used to provide electricity to remote homes, cabins, and isolated applications such as livestock water pumping, security lighting, roadside message boards, billboards, and other data sensors. The sun's energy can be used in many ways, such as heating water in homes. Solar water heaters are currently used in Arizona, Florida, and many other sunny parts of the United States. One popular use of solar energy is to heat private swimming pools.

The concept of solar energy is not new. In the 1920s, tens of thousands of solar water heaters were in use. Then, after large deposits of oil and natural gas were discovered in the western United States, and gas became a cheaper source of energy, solar water systems began to be replaced with heaters that burned fossil fuels, which then remained the principal source of heating.

With the high price of gas today, solar water heaters are now beginning to make a comeback. They can effectively heat water for use inside homes and businesses through the placement of panels on the roof of a building that contains water pipes. When the sun hits the panels and the pipes, the sunlight warms them, providing heat.

Solar energy is also used to make electricity. Some solar power stations use a highly curved mirror, called a parabolic trough, to focus the sunlight onto a pipe running down a central point above the curve of the mirror. The mirror focuses the sunlight to strike the pipe, which gets so hot that it boils water into steam. The steam is then used to

Solar energy applications: (a) A home that uses solar energy. A photovoltaic system provides power to the house and a solar hot water system provides hot water for domestic and space heating use. (b) A solar meter attached to a solar house, known as a "zero energy home." Such homes produce all the energy they need from photovoltaic systems, passive solar designs, geothermal heat pumps, compact fluorescent lighting, and high efficiency appliances. (c) Swimming pools can be heated using solar energy. A roof-mounted solar pool heating system on this house heats the swimming pool in the foreground. (d) A photovoltaic system consisting of 372 solar panels on the roof of the Williams Building, in Boston, Massachusetts. *(a, b, d, courtesy of U.S. Dept of Energy; c, courtesy of National Renewable Energy Laboratory, U.S. Dept. of Energy)*

turn a turbine that generates electricity. Some power plants utilize mirrors called heliostats that are able to move and turn to face the sun all day long.

In California's Mojave Desert, there is currently a solar thermal power plant that produces electricity for more than 350,000 homes. These types of facilities, as discussed in Chapter 3, require prolonged periods of clear skies. Because solar power plants cannot create energy on cloudy days, some solar plants have solved this problem by creating a "hybrid" technology. During the daytime, they use the Sun's energy. At night and on cloudy days, they burn natural gas to boil the water so that they can continue to make electricity.

Solar cells—or photovoltaic energy—are also used to change sunlight directly into electricity. Photovoltaic (PV) cells can be found on many small appliances, such as calculators and watches. They are even used on spacecraft. In fact, they were first developed in the 1950s for use on the U.S. space satellites. They are made of silicon—a special type of melted sand.

When sunlight strikes the solar cell, electrons are displaced and move toward the heated front surface of the cell. An electron imbalance is created between the front and back. When the two surfaces are joined by a connector—such as a wire—a current of electricity occurs between the negative and positive sides.

Individual solar cells are arranged together into a PV module and the modules are grouped together into an array (a cluster of solar cells) as mentioned previously. Some of the arrays are set on special tracking devices to follow sunlight all day long, maximizing the solar energy input.

The electricity from solar cells can be used directly in homes to power lights and appliances. Some homeowners choose to use these photovoltaic systems instead of the readily available commercial energy generated from fossil fuels. Right now, however, these systems are expensive to install and can be cost prohibitive.

Solar energy can also be used in business buildings to generate electricity. In addition, it has uses in remote applications where power lines

The Sacramento Municipal Utility District in California operates a photovoltaic array (foreground). Nuclear cooling towers are visible in the background. *(Photo by National Renewable Energy Laboratory)*

do not exist, such as to illuminate billboards along roads and to power the portable radar assemblies used by police departments to give drivers readouts of their current speed. Solar energy can also be stored in the batteries that operate emergency roadside cellular telephones. Some experimental cars also use PV cells by converting sunlight directly into energy to power electric motors on the car.

Photovoltaic research and development programs are currently looking at a technology that replaces existing roofing materials—such as shingles—with photovoltaic materials. The federal government is also dedicated to this research, and has presented the Million Solar Roofs Initiative to Congress to help this research and promote the use of "green" energy.

Some power production plants combine several types of alternative energy sources. For example, as shown in the photo above, a photovoltaic array can be used along with nuclear power.

IMPACTS ON THE ENVIRONMENT FROM ENERGY SOURCES

As we have seen, electricity can be created from several sources, such as natural gas, coal, oil, nuclear energy, municipal solid waste (garbage dumps), hydropower, solar power, geothermal sources, biomass, and wind. Although each of these represents a valuable resource in which to provide the energy critical to a functioning society, there are also impacts to the environment associated with each of these sources.

Natural Gas

At the power plant, the burning of natural gas produces nitrogen oxides and carbon dioxide (but in lower quantities than burning coal or oil). Methane may be emitted into the air when natural gas is not completely burned. The burning of natural gas in combustion turbines requires very little water, but natural gas-fired boiler and combined cycle systems do require water for cooling purposes. One disadvantage of this is that when power plants remove water from a lake or river, fish and other aquatic life can be harmed or killed. In addition, heat and pollutants build up in the water used in natural gas boilers and combined cycle systems. When the pollutants and heat reach certain levels, the water is often discharged into lakes or rivers. The Environmental Protection Agency (EPA) closely monitors this impact to keep it to a minimum.

The use of natural gas to create electricity does not produce substantial amounts of solid waste. There are some drawbacks to using natural gas, however, such as the fact that extraction of natural gas and the construction of power plants can destroy natural habitat for animals and plants. Possible land resource impacts include erosion, loss of soil productivity, and landslides.

Coal

When coal is burned, carbon dioxide, sulfur dioxide, nitrogen oxides, and mercury compounds are released. For that reason, coal-fired boilers are required to have control devices to reduce the emissions that are released. In addition, the processes of mining, cleaning, and transporting coal to the power plant generates additional emissions. Methane that is trapped in the coal is often vented during these processes to protect workers in the coal industry from inhaling the hazardous gas.

Large quantities of water are needed to remove **impurities** from coal when it is mined. Coal-fired power plants use large quantities of water for producing steam and for cooling. When coal-fired power plants remove water from a lake or river, fish and other aquatic life can be affected, as well as animals and people that depend on these aquatic resources.

Pollutants also build up in the water used in the power plant boiler and cooling system. If the water used in the power plant is discharged to a lake or river, the pollutants in the water can also harm fish and plants. In addition, if rain falls on coal stored in piles outside the power plant, the water that runs off these piles can flush heavy metals from the coal, such as arsenic and lead, into nearby bodies of water, which also threatens wildlife and the environment. Coal mining can also contaminate bodies of water with heavy metals when the water used to clean the coal is discharged back into the environment.

When coal is burned, it creates solid waste called ash, which is composed primarily of metal oxides and alkali. Coal can contain up to 10% ash. Solid waste is also created at coal mines when coal is cleaned and at power plants when air pollutants are removed from the stack gas. The majority of this waste is still deposited in landfills and abandoned mines, although practices have now been put in place to recycle them into useful products, such as cement and building materials. As people become more environmentally aware, this trend will lessen the environmental impacts generated from the use of coal.

Soil at coal-fired power plants can also become contaminated with various pollutants from the coal and take a long time to recover, even after the power plant closes down. Coal mining and processing also impacts the land. Surface mining disturbs larger areas than underground mining and can create eyesores for people living nearby. Because of this, mining companies often elect to mine the coal with conservation in mind. As they remove a section of overburden to access the coal, the overburden of the next section to be mined is used to fill in the open pit left from the previous section. In this way, reclamation practices are put into effect during the mining operation, not solely at the end. This process also allows the land to recover quicker, enabling native vegetation to repopulate the disturbed area.

Oil

Burning oil at power plants produces several emissions, such as nitrogen oxides, sulfur dioxide, carbon dioxide, methane, and mercury compounds. The amounts can vary depending on the sulfur and mercury content of the oil that is burned. Emissions from natural gas or diesel are also produced by the equipment that is used in the oil drilling, production, and transportation of oil resources.

Oil-fired power plants use large quantities of water for steam production and cooling. Like other forms of energy, when oil-fired power plants remove water from a lake or river, fish and other aquatic life can be harmed or killed. The drilling of oil requires water to remove obstructions from the well. Refineries release treated wastewater, which can contain pollutants, into streams and other bodies of water. The waste water can also be hotter than the lakes and streams where it is emitted, thereby harming the fish and plants that live there.

Drilling can also cause underground water supplies to become contaminated with oil. Oil refining produces wastewater sludge and other solid waste that can contain high levels of metals and toxic compounds. When oil is burned at power plants, residues that are not completely burned can accumulate, forming yet another source of solid waste that must be disposed of. The construction of large oil-fired power plants can also destroy plant and animal habitat. When oil spills occur on land, soils are also harmed and processes to clean them up can take many years.

Nuclear Energy

Nuclear power plants do not emit carbon dioxide, sulfur dioxide, or nitrogen oxides. However, fossil fuel emissions are associated with the uranium mining and uranium enrichment process as well as the transportation of the uranium fuel to the nuclear power plant, so the emissions and impacts that apply to burning fossil fuels also indirectly affect the use of nuclear energy.

Nuclear power plants use large quantities of water for steam production and cooling. When nuclear power plants remove water from a lake or river for steam production and cooling, fish and other aquatic life can be adversely affected in the same way that other energy resources impact water bodies. Water pollutants, such as heavy metals and salts, build up in the water used in the nuclear power plant systems. These pollutants also negatively impact water quality and aquatic life. Although the nuclear reactor is radioactive, the water discharged from the power plant is not, because it never comes in contact with any of the radioactive materials. However, waste generated from uranium mining operations and rainwater runoff can contaminate both ground water and surface water resources with heavy metals and traces of radioactive uranium.

Nuclear power plants must be shut down every year and a half to two years in order to remove and replace the "spent" uranium fuel. This spent fuel has released most of its energy as a result of the fission process and has become radioactive waste.

According to the U.S. Department of Energy, all of the nuclear power plants in the United States together produce about 2,000 metric tons per year of radioactive waste. Currently, the radioactive waste is stored at the nuclear plants at which it is generated, either in steel-lined, concrete vaults filled with water or in above-ground steel or steel-reinforced concrete containers with steel inner canisters. The Department of Energy is currently interested in a permanent central repository at Yucca Mountain in Nevada for all nuclear waste. The repository could begin to accept waste by 2012, if approved. This issue has created much controversy in the American Southwest.

In addition to the fuel waste, much of the equipment in the nuclear power plants becomes contaminated with radiation and will become radioactive waste after the plant is closed. These wastes have extremely long half-lives (the time required for one-half the atoms of a given

Nuclear energy impacts: (a) A spent fuel cask used at a nuclear power plant. Nuclear waste is packaged and transported in casks such as this one. (b) Yucca Mountain in Nevada is under consideration to serve as a geologic repository for the nation's spent nuclear fuel and high-level radioactive waste. It is 100 miles (160 km) northwest of Las Vegas in an isolated part of Nye County. (c) Metal boxes containing radioactive waste are stacked in an engineered trench at the Savannah River disposal site in South Carolina. When all available space is used up, soil and a protective covering for erosion control will be placed on top of the waste containers. (d) A computer-guided robot is used at the Savannah River Laboratory to detect cracks in the walls of nuclear reactors. *(Photos courtesy of U.S. Department of Energy)*

The Chernobyl Nuclear Disaster

One of the worst impacts a nuclear power plant can have on the environment and human life is a radioactive accident. In the early morning hours of April 26, 1986, a testing error caused an explosion at the Chernobyl nuclear power station in northern Ukraine. During a radioactive fire that burned for 10 days, 190 tons of toxic materials were expelled into the atmosphere. The wind blew 70% of the radioactive materials into the neighboring country of Belarus. Almost 20 years later, the people of Belarus continue to suffer medically, economically, environmentally, and socially from the effects of the disaster. The following are the facts from the accident:

- The explosion of the reactor at Chernobyl released 100 times more radiation than the atomic bombs dropped on Hiroshima and Nagasaki.

- At the time of the accident, about seven million people lived in contaminated territories, including three million children.

- About 5.5 million people continue to live in contaminated zones today.

- Although 31 people died as a direct result of the Chernobyl disaster, more than 25,000 people have since died from diseases such as lung cancer, leukemia, and cardiovascular disease.

- In Belarus, 21% of prime farmland still remains dangerously contaminated from decaying components of plutonium.

- The economic damages to Belarus over a 30-year period after the accident is estimated to reach $235 billion.

- After the Chernobyl accident, almost 400,000 people were forced to leave their homes for their own safety. Over 2,000 towns and villages were bulldozed to the ground, and hundreds more stand vacant.

- Nearly 97% of the radioactive materials from the Chernobyl plant remain inside a hastily constructed concrete shell. According to a 2003 report by the Russian Atomic Energy Minister, Alexander Rumyantsev, the shell is in danger of collapsing at any time. A new shelter is scheduled to be completed in 2009; it is hoped that it will safely contain Chernobyl for the next 100 years.

Source: Chernobyl Children's Project International

amount of a radioactive substance to decay) and will remain radioactive for many thousands of years. For this reason, the use of nuclear energy has been a highly controversial subject for many years.

The processing of uranium also produces radioactive wastes that must be adequately stored and isolated to minimize the risk of radioactive release. The management, packaging, transport, and disposal of this waste is strictly regulated and carefully controlled by the U.S. Nuclear Regulatory Commission.

The construction of nuclear power plants can destroy natural habitat for animals and plants or contaminate land with toxic by-products. Another drawback is that the storage of radioactive waste may also keep future re-use of the land from being possible, due to potential health risks.

Municipal Solid Waste

Burning municipal solid waste (MSW)—or garbage—produces nitrogen oxides and sulfur dioxide as well as trace amounts of toxic pollutants, such as mercury compounds and **dioxins**. Although MSW power plants do emit carbon dioxide—the primary greenhouse gas—some of it is considered to be part of the Earth's natural carbon cycle, because the plants and trees that make up the paper and food waste being burned initially removed carbon dioxide from the air while they were growing.

The variation in the composition of MSW does affect the emissions impact. For example, if MSW containing batteries and tires is burned, the toxic materials contained in them can be released into the air causing environmental impacts. A variety of air pollution control technologies are used today to reduce toxic air pollutants from MSW power plants.

Power plants that burn MSW are normally smaller than fossil fuel power plants but typically require a similar amount of water per unit of electricity generated. Like many other types of energy processing, when water is removed from a lake or river, fish and other aquatic life can be killed.

MSW power plants also discharge used water. Pollutants build up in the water used in the power plant boiler and cooling system. In addition, the cooling water is considerably warmer when it is discharged than when it was taken in. These water pollutants and the higher temperature of the discharged water can negatively affect water quality.

When MSW is burned, it reduces the creation of new landfills, thereby helping the environment. MSW combustion, however, does create ash (a solid waste), which can contain any of the elements that were originally present in the waste. Because ash and other residues from MSW operations may contain toxic materials, the power plant wastes must be tested regularly to assure that the wastes are safely disposed of to prevent toxic substances from migrating into ground-water supplies. Depending on state and local restrictions, non-hazardous ash may be disposed of in a MSW landfill or recycled for use in roads, parking lots, or daily covering for sanitary landfills. MSW power plants, like fossil fuel power plants, also require land for equipment and fuel storage.

Hydropower

Hydropower's air emissions are negligible because no fuels are burned in the production of electricity. However, if a large amount of vegetation is growing along the riverbed when a dam is built, it can decay in the lake that is created, causing the buildup and release of methane. Hydropower often requires the use of dams, which can greatly affect the flow of rivers, thereby altering ecosystems and affecting the wildlife and people who depend on those waters. Often, water at the bottom of the lake created by a dam is inhospitable to fish because it is much colder and oxygen-poor compared with water at the top. When this colder, oxygen-poor water is released into the river, it can kill fish living downstream that are accustomed to warmer, oxygen-rich water. Eroded material from upstream sources also collects in dams, and over time, they become filled with huge deposits of silt that must be dredged. Nutrients and stream load (sediments) necessary for the health and balance of the waterway, that would have naturally been carried down river, become trapped in the reservoir behind the dam. This can have negative effects. For example, sediment-starved water exiting the dam has a higher potential to cause erosion and other damage downstream, upsetting delicate ecological balances. In addition, some dams withhold water and then release it all at once, causing the river downstream to suddenly flood. This action can disrupt plant and wildlife habitats and affect drinking water supplies.

The construction of hydropower plants can alter sizable portions of land when dams are constructed and lakes are created, flooding land that may have once served as wildlife habitat, farmland, and scenic retreat. For example, many beautiful waterways, once enjoyed for rafting and other recreational activities, are destroyed when reservoirs take their place. In the American Southwest, many archaeological sites have been submerged in the reservoirs created by dams. This presents a controversial issue because pieces of history become lost. Hydroelectric dams can cause erosion along the riverbed upstream and downstream, which can further disturb wildlife ecosystems and fish populations.

Solar Energy

The environmental impacts of solar energy are minimal. Air emissions associated with generating electricity from solar technologies are negligible because no fuels are burned. Water may be used in solar-thermal technologies to create steam, but the water can be re-used after it has been condensed from steam back into water. Solar-thermal technologies do not produce any substantial amount of solid waste while creating electricity, either. The biggest impact from thermal-solar power production is that they require a significant amount of land. Although solar energy installations do not damage the land, they do prevent it from being used for other purposes.

Geothermal

Air emissions generated from geothermal technologies are negligible because no fuels are combusted in this process. Geothermal power plants usually re-inject the hot water that they remove from the ground back into wells. However, geothermal power plants can possibly cause groundwater contamination when drilling wells and extracting hot water or steam. This type of contamination can be prevented with proper management techniques.

Geothermal technologies do not produce a substantial amount of solid waste while creating electricity. Geothermal power plants typically require the use of less land than fossil fuel power plants. However, if water is not reinjected into the ground after use to maintain pressure underground, it may cause sinking of land at the surface.

Biomass

Biomass energy sources include trees, organic garbage, agricultural waste, fuel crops, garden waste, sewage sludge, manure, cornhusks, rice hulls, peanut shells, grass clippings, leaves, and other organic materials. Biomass power plants emit nitrogen oxides and a small amount of sulfur dioxide. The amounts emitted depend on the type of biomass that is burned and the type of generator that is used. Although the burning of biomass also produces carbon dioxide—the primary greenhouse gas—as an emission, similar to the burning of MSW, it is considered to be part of the natural carbon cycle of the Earth. (The carbon dioxide released equals the initial amount of carbon dioxide absorbed while the biomass was alive.) Biomass contains much less sulfur and nitrogen than coal; therefore, when biomass is cofired with coal, sulfur dioxide and nitrogen oxide emissions are lower than when coal is burned alone, presenting a more environmentally sound method of energy production. Biomass power plants require the use of water, because the boilers burning the biomass need water for steam production and for cooling. If this water is used over and over again, the amount of water needed is reduced.

Similar to fossil fuel power plants, biomass power plants have pollutants that build up in the water used in the boiler and cooling system. The water used for cooling is much warmer when it is returned to the lake or river than it was when removed. Similar to other energy processing technologies, pollutants in the water and the water's higher temperature can harm fish and plants in the lake or river.

The burning of biomass in boilers creates ash that must be disposed of properly, but fortunately, it normally contains extremely low levels of hazardous elements. Generating electricity from biomass can affect land resources in different ways. For example, some biomass power plants require large areas of land for equipment and fuel storage. Biomass grown for fuel purposes requires large areas of land and, over time, can deplete the soil of nutrients. Fuel crops must be managed so that they stabilize the soil, reduce erosion, provide wildlife habitat, and serve recreational purposes.

Landfill Gas

Burning landfill gas produces nitrogen oxide emissions as well as trace amounts of toxic materials. The amount of these emissions can vary widely, depending on the waste from which the landfill gas was created. Similar to MSW and biomass methodologies, the carbon dioxide released from the burning landfill gas is considered to be a part of the natural carbon cycle of the Earth. Engines or combustion turbines burning landfill gas have very little or no water discharges. The collection of landfill gas involves drilling wells into landfills, which does not affect local bodies of water. Landfill gas technologies also do not produce any substantial amount of solid waste while creating electricity.

Burning landfill gas to produce electricity has little impact on land resources. While the equipment used to burn the landfill gas and generate electricity does require space, it can be located on land already occupied by the existing landfill, thereby avoiding any additional use of land.

Wind

Air emissions associated with generating electricity from wind technology are negligible because no fuels are combusted. Wind turbines in areas with little rainfall may require the use of a small amount of water in order to clean dirt and insects off the turbine blades so that they do

The research program at this radiobiology laboratory aims to determine human health hazards from exposure to energy-related pollutants, such as the pollutants associated with combustion of fossil fuels. *(Courtesy of U.S. Department of Energy)*

not hamper turbine performance. Wind technologies also do not produce any substantial amount of solid waste while creating electricity.

Wind turbines generally require the use of land, although they may also be sited offshore. In fact, current technology is developing ways to put large wind farms in ocean coastal areas. Land around wind turbines can be used for other purposes, such as the grazing of cattle or farming.

Large wind farms cause aesthetic concerns because some people do not like looking at them. Noise from the turbines can also be an issue, but new blade designs are being developed to reduce the amount of noise that is currently generated. Bird and bat mortality has been an issue at some wind farms. Improvements to wind turbine technologies have helped with this problem. Improperly installed wind farms may create soil erosion problems.

No matter what method is used to generate energy, health concerns are a high priority. Whether it is radioactive exposure to nuclear energy or exposure to hazardous materials when mining commodities such as coal, health hazard research is an important component of any energy production site.

THE IMPORTANCE OF ENERGY

This chapter explores some of the many goods and services that energy resources provide. Several have already been discussed in detail throughout the previous chapters, such as fuel—from petroleum and biomass sources—for heat and transportation; and the generation of electricity, a secondary energy source, from many different types of resources, such as petroleum, geothermal energy, water, solar energy, coal, uranium, and wind energy. Previous chapters have also discussed energy's role in the advancement of civilization and the provision of human comfort and the resulting improvements in people's lifestyles, as well as its significant role in the Industrial Revolution and its use in communication and technology.

This chapter discusses a sampling of the multitude of important petroleum and biomass energy products that are used every day; employment and research opportunities generated from energy resources; nuclear medicine; practical applications of the electromagnetic spectrum, such as satellite data, remote sensing applications, global positioning systems, and microwave cooking; and finally, space exploration and military applications.

PETROLEUM AND BIOMASS PRODUCTS

People have used petroleum for thousands of years. The Bible mentions that Noah used a solid form of petroleum called pitch in building the Ark. The ancient Egyptians coated mummies with pitch. Pitch was also used to build walls and pave streets in Babylon. American Indians used crude oil for fuel and medicine hundreds of years before the first European settlers arrived. In the 1850s, oil was used as a cure for many ailments. American history tells that frontiersman Kit Carson sold oil as axle grease to the pioneers. A major breakthrough in the use of petroleum occurred in the late 1840s, when a Canadian geologist, named Abraham Gesner, discovered kerosene—a fuel that could be distilled from coal or oil. Kerosene became widely used for lighting lamps, causing it to quickly rise in value.

During the 1800s, kerosene was the chief product of the petroleum industry. Ironically, refiners considered gasoline a useless by-product and often dumped it into creeks and rivers. Then, about 1900, two events dramatically changed this situation—electric lights began to replace kerosene lamps, and the automobile was invented. The demand for kerosene declined just as an enormous market for gasoline opened up.

World War I (1914–1918) created a tremendous demand for petroleum fuels to power ships and airplanes. Fuels became as important as ammunition. After the war, the use of petroleum brought about big changes on farms. More and more farmers began to operate tractors and other equipment powered by oil, replacing the extensive use of animals for plowing and other types of work. Petroleum also provided the asphalt needed to build roads in rural areas, increasing farmers' access to market and subsequent increased economic growth.

During World War II (1939–1945), the American oil industry began to increase production and develop specialized products. Huge quantities of oil were produced and converted into fuels and lubricants. New refining processes increased the output of high-octane aviation gasoline. The United States was able to provide 80% of the aviation gasoline used by the Allies during the war. American refineries also manufactured butadiene, which was used to make synthetic rubber; toluene (an ingredient in TNT explosives); medicinal oils to treat the wounded; and many other military necessities.

Some of the petroleum technology perfected during the war became the basis for peacetime industry. Today, according to the American Petroleum Institute, there are more than 3,000 synthetic products made from fossil fuels.

All plastic is made from petroleum products, and it is used almost everywhere: houses, cars, toys, computers, furniture, clothing, and a multitude of other uses. Asphalt used in road construction is also a petroleum product, as is the synthetic rubber in tires. Paraffin wax comes from petroleum, as do fertilizer, pesticides, herbicides, detergents, phonograph records, photographic film, furniture packaging materials, surfboards, paints, and artificial fibers used in clothing, upholstery, and carpet backing.

Petroleum products fall into three major categories: (1) fuels, such as motor gasoline and diesel; (2) finished non-fuel products, such as solvents and lubricating oils; and (3) feedstock for the petrochemical industry. Petrochemical feedstock is used to produce many items. It is what is converted to the basic chemical building blocks and intermediates used to produce plastics, synthetic rubber, synthetic fibers, drugs, and detergents.

Not as widely used as petroleum products are the renewable bio-based products (also called bioproducts). These are products created from plant- or crop-based resources, such as agricultural crops and crop residues, forestry, pastures, leaves, and rangeland material. Like petroleum, bioproducts can be used to manufacture a wide variety of goods, such as plastics, natural rubber, paint, adhesives, drugs, and solvents. Bioproducts are also major sources for fuels, such as ethanol. Currently these plant resources provide only 5% of manufacturing materials, but scientists believe they will continue to gain importance in manufacturing in the future.

A clean air fuel pump containing 85% ethanol—a bioproduct made from corn. *(Courtesy of U.S. Department of Energy)*

Companies from the chemical, life sciences, forestry, and agricultural communities are involved in establishing the renewable bioproducts industry. Their activities range from genetic engineering of new plant species to development of new technologies and processes for converting plants into useful industrial products. DuPont recently developed a bio-based method that uses corn instead of petroleum-based processes to produce a new polymer to be used in clothing, carpets, and automobile interiors. Currently, production of bio-based textile fabrics, polymers, adhesives, lubricants, soy-based inks, and other products is estimated at more than 12 billion pounds (5.4 billion kg) per year.

EMPLOYMENT AND RESEARCH OPPORTUNITIES

Energy resources provide an abundance of employment and research opportunities. Millions of people around the world are employed to find or produce petroleum, ship and refine it, and manufacture and market the many products made from it. The refineries where crude oil is processed are large and complex—they occupy many acres of land and employ thousands of people. Jobs are provided for people from the mining phase to the refining and distributing phases, creating a very important employment sector in United States commerce.

According to data from the American Petroleum Institute, America's 187,000 service stations are a huge network of small businesses. Maintenance of these businesses employs many people. As people become more environmentally oriented, the responsibilities of proper maintenance also employ many people. In order to prevent contamination of soil and groundwater, underground storage tanks and their associated piping are monitored for leaks, are built to withstand corrosion, and are equipped to safeguard against spills and overfilling. Scientists and engineers must design this equipment to be environmentally safe.

In addition, with the growing importance of bioproducts, the potential growth of positions in research and development is enormous. Currently, scientists all around the world hold research positions in the energy industry, as humans try to find new energy resources to replace, or help cut down, the use of nonrenewable petroleum products.

NUCLEAR MEDICINE

Electromagnetic energy is used regularly in the medical field in the form of X-rays and other diagnostic imaging systems. The branch of medicine that uses electromagnetic energy is called nuclear medicine.

Nuclear medicine imaging—also called radionuclide scanning—is an excellent diagnostic tool because it shows not only the anatomy (structure) of an organ or body part, but the function of the organ as well. This functional information allows nuclear medicine to diagnose certain diseases and various medical conditions much sooner than other medical imaging examinations, which provide only anatomic (structural) information about an organ. Nuclear medicine can be valuable in the early diagnosis, treatment, and prevention of numerous medical conditions.

When a doctor takes an X-ray, the radiation comes out of the X-ray system and then passes through the patient's body before being detected and recorded onto film or by a computer. Nuclear medicine uses the opposite approach—a radioactive material is introduced into the patient and is then detected by a machine called a gamma camera. The radiation, which is emitted by the body during the nuclear medicine imaging, is made up of gamma rays. Gamma rays are similar to X-rays, but they have a shorter wavelength.

Different tissue types absorb the radionuclides (radioactive nuclides) at different rates. The amount of radiation that is taken up and then emitted by a specific body part is linked to the metabolic activity (cellular function) of the organ or tissue. For example, cells that are dividing rapidly—like cancer tissue cells—may be seen as "hot spots" of metabolic activity on a nuclear medicine scan, because they absorb more of the radionuclide.

This specialized technology has several beneficial applications. It can be used for bone scanning to detect cancer. It is also a valuable tool in the diagnosis and treatment of heart disease. Nuclear medicine can provide excellent images of the beating heart and blood vessels, thereby allowing doctors more accurate diagnostic abilities.

ELECTROMAGNETIC SPECTRUM APPLICATIONS

Electromagnetic energy is all the energy that comes from the Sun. This energy travels through space from the Sun to the Earth and is composed of many different wavelengths. The shortest wavelengths in the spectrum are gamma rays, X-rays, and ultraviolet rays. Humans cannot see this energy. X-rays are what doctors and dentists use to image bones and teeth.

As the wavelengths get longer, visible light occurs. These are the wavelengths humans can see, but they constitute a very tiny portion of the entire spectrum. Visible light can be broken into all the colors of the rainbow: red, orange, yellow, green, blue, indigo, and violet.

Wavelengths that are larger in size than those of the visible **spectrum** cannot be seen by humans. These longer wavelengths include infrared radiation, microwave radiation, and radio wavelengths. Scientists refer to these groups of wavelengths as bands—the blue band, green band, red band, infrared band, microwave band, radio band, and so forth.

Electromagnetic energy can be used for a multitude of things—its applications are used every day by humans. Examples of valuable applications include microwave ovens, remote sensing (satellite imaging), global positioning systems, communication satellites, radio transmission, and cellular phones.

Microwave Ovens

Microwaves are very short waves of electromagnetic energy that travel at the speed of light (186,282 miles per second, or 299,780 km per second). Uses for microwaves include the relay of distant telephone signals, television programs, and computer information across the Earth or to a satellite in space. One of the most familiar applications of microwaves is their use in microwave ovens as an energy source to cook food.

Every microwave oven contains a magnetron—a tube in which electrons are affected by magnetic and electric fields in such a way as to produce micro-wavelength radiation. The microwave energy inter-acts with the molecules in food. All wave energy changes polarity from positive to negative with each cycle of the wave. In microwaves, these polarity changes happen millions of times every second. Food mole-cules—especially the molecules of water—have a positive and negative end in the same way a magnet has a north and a south polarity.

As the microwaves generated from the magnetron bombard the food, they cause the polar molecules to rotate at the same frequency millions of times a second. All this agitation creates molecular friction, which, in turn, heats up the food. Microwave ovens use alternating cur-rent (AC) to create the frictional heat.

Remote Sensing

Remote sensing is the science of collecting information about some-thing without having to be in physical contact with it. When study-ing the Earth, a common platform for obtaining images and data is through the use of satellites. Satellites allow the Earth's surface, atmo-sphere, and oceans to be observed from space. Satellites can "image" the Earth using different wavelengths of the electromagnetic spectrum. Each of these different wavelength bands can give unique information about the surface of the Earth.

For example, systems that collect data in the green band spec-trum allow scientists to determine the health of vegetation. The shorter wavelengths of infrared bands allow analysts to determine the differences between different types of vegetation, such as plants, trees, grasses, shrubs, as well as which specific species they are. The longer—or thermal-infrared wavelengths—can identify objects that are warmer than their surroundings. The resulting images are often used by search and rescue units to locate lost hikers. They are also used by utility companies to determine how much heat a house is losing. This imagery serves as a way to "see" which parts of the house need better insulation. In these images, the brighter colors (yellow, orange, and red) indicate that more heat is escaping than in the darker colors (blue and green).

Heat escaping from a house can be detected through the use of thermal infrared scanners. The orange, yellow, and red areas indicate where the most energy is escaping. Double-pane insulated windows can reduce energy loss. In homes where heat escapes through the roof and walls, more insulation is required to prevent energy loss. *(Photos courtesy of U.S. Department of Energy, National Renewable Energy Laboratory)*

Other infrared bands allow geologists to look at rock formation on the Earth's surface and find mineral deposits. When the radar energy wavelengths are used, structural features can be seen. Radar can also "see" through clouds so that continually cloudy areas, such as tropical rain forests, can still be studied by scientists.

Satellite imagery using the Sun's energy can be used for many purposes, such as classifying soils and vegetation; monitoring the health of forests and agricultural fields; mapping roads; studying wetlands; mapping wildlife habitat; detecting changes on the surface of the Earth over time; and monitoring the health of wildlands, rangelands, and wilderness.

Global Positioning System

A global positioning system (GPS) is a system of satellites established and maintained by the U.S. Department of Defense. These satellites can also be used by civilians for many applications, such as mapping, navigation, survey, and for tracking hiking paths through remote areas. The GPS satellites provide accurate navigational and positional locations. It is the only system that can determine a GPS user's exact position on the Earth. This system works everywhere on the planet, at any time (day or night) and in any type of weather.

The 24 satellites in this system transmit energy signals that anyone with a GPS receiver can detect. GPS is one of the most exciting and revolutionary developments created in modern times. The GPS satellites each take 12 hours to orbit the Earth, each satellite broadcasting its signal. A ground unit receives the signal, which travels at the speed of light. The difference between the time the signal was sent and the time it was received goes into a calculation of distance. A standard GPS can pinpoint a location anywhere on the surface of the Earth within 300 feet (91 m); an upper-grade GPS has a much higher level of accuracy and can locate points within a few inches (cm).

This technology has been a valuable asset to the U.S. military. Troops relied heavily on GPS during Operation Desert Storm to navigate through the vast expanses of featureless desert. GPS enabled troops to maneuver through blinding sandstorms and at night when the enemy could not.

Besides the military, many other organization use GPS extensively—police, fire, and emergency medical service units; delivery trucks; wildlife biologists; and mapping units. Private-vehicle tracking programs, such as On-Star, use this technology so that an individual's precise location is known in case of an emergency.

Communication Satellites

Communication satellites are used to transmit telephone and television signals. In 1963, the necessary rocket booster power was available to put a satellite high enough into orbit so that it could be used to transmit data 24 hours a day.

Today, there are approximately 150 communications satellites in orbit around the Earth. Satellites are also able to relay signals to each other, making it possible for thousands of phone calls to be made between almost any two points on the Earth, as well as live television transmission between virtually any two points on Earth. Antennas transmit the energy signals.

Once in orbit, the satellite must generate all of its own power. That power is usually generated by large solar panels covered with solar cells, which convert sunlight into electricity. Satellites must also have a way to function when the Sun is not visible—usually because the Earth is passing between the satellite and the Sun. This requires that the satellite have batteries on board that can supply the required power for the necessary time and then recharge by the time of the next eclipse of the sun.

Radios

Radio waves are part of the electromagnetic spectrum. Radio stations use antennas to **radiate** energy preferentially in specific directions. Radio stations keep from interfering with each other's signals by broadcasting at slightly different energy wavelengths in the spectrum.

Other items that utilize this electromagnetic energy include cellular phones, heat sealers, vinyl welders, high-frequency welders, induction heaters, communications transmitters, radar transmitters, microwave drying equipment, and glue curing equipment.

SPACE EXPLORATION AND MILITARY APPLICATIONS

Energy sources are also critical to the U.S. space program and the military. On October 1, 1958, the National Aeronautics and Space Administration (NASA) was formed. It was the beginning of a rich history of unique scientific technological achievements in human space flight, aeronautics, space science, and space applications.

NASA's first big-profile program was Project Mercury, an effort to learn if humans could survive in space, followed by Project Gemini, which built upon Project Mercury's successes and used spacecraft built for two astronauts. NASA's human space flight efforts then extended to the moon with Project Apollo, culminating in 1969 when the Apollo 11 mission first put humans on the lunar surface. After the Skylab and Apollo-Soyuz Test Projects of the early and mid-1970s, NASA's human space flight efforts again resumed in 1981 with the space shuttle program that continues today to help build the International Space Station (ISS) and conduct a multitude of space exploration and development tasks.

Through the use of energy, NASA has also launched a number of significant scientific probes such as the *Pioneer* and *Voyager* spacecraft that have explored the Moon, the planets, and other areas of the solar system. NASA has been able to launch several spacecraft to investigate Mars. The Hubble Space Telescope and other spacecraft have enabled scientists to make a number of significant astronomical discoveries about our universe.

The ISS is a manned space station. In 1998, the first two modules were launched and joined together in orbit. The first crew arrived in 2000. Scientists from many countries occupy the ISS to conduct a wide variety of experiments, such as energy-related studies of the electro-magnetic spectrum and aerodynamics. Similar to orbiting satellites, the ISS uses a solar array for energy generation.

Space experimentation has not only given us valuable information about outer space, but many of the experiments and discoveries made

(a) A space shuttle on the launchpad at Cape Canaveral in Florida. (b) A space shuttle immediately after launch. (c) The International Space Station. Note the solar array panels used as an energy source. *(Courtesy of NASA)*

The military's B-2 Spirit is a multi-role bomber capable of delivering both conventional and nuclear munitions. Known as the stealth bomber, it is virtually undetectable by radar systems. *(Courtesy of the U.S. Department of Defense)*

on space missions have had a direct impact on items that humans use every day. For example, NASA research has resulted in improved athletic shoe materials, more accurate and aerodynamic golf balls, more efficient home insulation, faster computer processors, fogless ski goggles, lighter helicopters, energy-saving air conditioners, and many other useful products and inventions.

Energy resources have also played a critical role in the development of military technology. Energy resources have been an integral part in technological advancement, especially from World War I to the present. Many sophisticated aircraft have been developed over the decades and a variety of weapons have been engineered. One of the most recent inventions in aircraft design is the B-2 Spirit. First introduced in 1988, it is the U.S. Air Force's (USAF) "stealth bomber"—capable of getting past sophisticated air-defense shields without detection from enemy forces. The bomber was a milestone in the United States' bomber modernization program. It is the most expensive plane ever built—up to $2.2 billion for each plane. It has the ability to fly to any point in the world within hours. Its unique profile comes from its "flying wing" construction; the leading edges of the wings are angled at 33 degrees and the trailing edge has a double-W shape.

An assessment published by the USAF showed that two B-2s armed with precision weaponry can do the job of 75 conventional aircraft. The bomber has a new radar-absorbent coating to preserve its stealth characteristics. The new material, known as Alternate High-Frequency Material (AHFM), is sprayed on by four independently controlled robots. The B-2 made its first flight on July 17, 1989, and entered the USAF operational fleet in 1993.

MANAGEMENT OF ENERGY RESOURCES

dvanced societies today require high levels of energy—energy that is readily available when and where it is needed. There are very few things in developed countries that do not require energy—buildings, cars, computers, electronic devices, buses, planes, trains, lighting, heating, video games, theme parks, movies, TV, music, and stereos are just a few of the things we depend on energy for. Because energy is such a critical component to life, like any valuable asset, it must be managed properly in order to ensure the best use of the resource.

As cities and populations grow, increased energy demands are also created. If energy sources are not proactively monitored, they may not be available when they are most needed. For example, hospitals must have an alternate energy source available in case of an electrical outage emergency. Fuel for cars must be available. If there was a massive shortage of fuel, it would impact every phase of the economy—people would lose their mobility, truckers would not be able to deliver food to grocery stores, flights would be cancelled, people would be unable to travel to work, and so on—a frightening scenario at best. All aspects of business would be negatively affected, as would society.

One of the best ways to manage energy resources is by conserving, recycling, and using renewable components. With recycling, it takes much less energy to reconvert the product than to manufacture the same product from all new components. It takes a lot of energy to initially manufacture common products like glass, aluminum, metal, paper, and plastic. Recycling saves energy and money.

Proper and conservative management practices are critical. This chapter outlines the practical management of energy in the short- and long-term in order to guarantee it will be available. It also presents the critical role the federal government plays in promoting energy conservation for itself, private industry, and private homeowners. It discusses many of the ongoing research and development projects, such as the Biomass Program, the Building Technologies Program, FreedomCAR and Vehicle Technologies Program, Industrial Technologies Program, the Geothermal Technologies Program, and the Solar Energy Technologies Program. It then outlines the challenges of managing the many uses of the land and the concerns scientists have about the conflict between wildlife habitat and energy mining areas. Finally, it addresses oil spills and their serious environmental impacts.

FEDERAL ENERGY MANAGEMENT

The federal government spends about $10 billion each year on energy and using products and services for its buildings, operation, and transportation. As the largest energy consumer in the United States—and the world's largest volume buyer of energy-related products—the federal government has both an opportunity and a responsibility to lead by example with smart energy management practices. By promoting energy efficiency and the use of renewable energy resources, the federal government can **conserve** energy, save taxpayer dollars, reduce pollution, conserve natural resources, and demonstrate leadership with responsible, cleaner energy sources.

Today's energy and facility managers need to be up to date on all the latest energy and water technologies in order to make choices that are cost-effective, energy smart, environmentally sound, and reliable in the management of energy resources. They must have the latest information concerning renewable, distributed energy and combined heat and power technologies. Facility managers must operate their buildings as efficiently as possible in order to have sustainable operations.

Effective management also helps increase the nation's energy security. Renewable energy can supply a naturally occurring, continual flow of energy, at or near the place where the energy is used. This can be important to energy managers who have to make sure their facilities will keep operating even if utility power is disrupted by reductions in supplies or national emergencies.

According to the U.S. Department of Energy, there are several reasons why the government promotes the use of renewable energy—such as reliable power supplies, more power available for peak-use periods, fewer (or no) greenhouse gases, lower risk of fuel spills in environmentally sensitive locations, less need for imported fuel, lower utility bills, reduced operational costs, and greater price stability in an uncertain energy economy.

As with managers of any other natural resource, energy managers strive to create a sustainable environmental stewardship with the land. Sustainable development and management allows a society to survive, thrive, and advance in a way that balances the social, economic, and environmental needs of current and future generations. Both short- and long-term goals must be considered.

There are many management practices that enable this to happen. Waste prevention and recycling is important in positive energy management. Many of the items that end up in the municipal landfills (garbage dumps) can be reduced, reused, or recycled. The best way to manage waste is to (1) prevent it by reducing and reusing materials when possible; (2) recycle, including composting; or (3) incinerate (burn) it.

Effective water efficiency measures can save millions of taxpayer dollars, and should be an integral part of every energy management program. This is because water requires a significant energy input for treatment, pumping, heating, and process uses.

Another way to reduce the impact of waste is to use environmentally preferable products and materials. It is also wise to look at the "whole building" design when developing a management plan that combines the architectural and engineered features of the building in relation to its environment. This can include using landscaping to provide shade from the sun and using the natural contour of the land to provide cooling/heating in subterranean levels. Many products on the market today are designed to be energy-efficient products: Desktop computers, laptop computers, monitors, printers, scanners, fax machines, TVs, VCRs, DVD players, stereos, and microwave ovens are available with low standby power mode and sleep mode. These products are commercially available to everyone; they are usually marked with the ENERGY STAR logo—meaning they are products identified by the federal government to be in the top 25% of the most energy-efficient products on the market. Energy Star is a government-backed program that helps businesses and individuals protect the environment through superior energy efficiency.

"Standby power" refers to the electricity used by electrical products when they are switched off or not performing their primary purpose. Products with low standby power can save a substantial amount of money over their lifetime. Fortunately, products with low standby power do not cost more to purchase.

"Sleep mode" is another energy-saving feature available on products. All Energy Star–labeled computers, monitors, copiers, printers, and fax machines will switch into a low-power sleep mode after a specified period of nonuse. When needed, these devices return automatically to the active mode. "Standby mode" differs from sleep mode because the user—not the machine itself—generally switches off the device and must manually turn it back on. The only devices that do not consume standby power are those with a switch that physically breaks the circuit.

Another important way to manage energy is through "green purchasing." Green purchasing involves buying products made from recycled materials, environmentally friendly products and services, bio-based products, energy- and water-efficient products, alternate fuel vehicles, products using renewable energy, and alternatives to hazardous or toxic chemicals.

According to the U.S. Department of Energy, inadequate maintenance of energy-using systems is a major cause of energy waste. If equipment becomes rundown from lack of servicing and maintenance, energy losses from steam, water and air leaks, uninsulated lines, or defective controls are often considerable. Good maintenance practices can generate substantial energy savings and should be considered a resource, because it is less expensive to monitor and maintain equipment with a planned schedule than to wait until it breaks down.

Many energy-efficient buildings today have computer-based, digitally controlled systems—or Direct Digital Control (DDC). DDC systems function by measuring various system variables (such as temperature), processing those variables (comparing a measured temperature to a desired set point), and then signaling a terminal device (air damper/mixing box) to respond. DDC systems can respond quicker and with more accuracy to a given input, thereby saving both energy and money.

THE BIOMASS PROGRAM

A primary goal of the National Energy Policy is to increase energy supplies using a more diverse mix of existing resources available in the country and to reduce the dependence on imported oil. The U.S. Department of Energy's Biomass Program develops technology for conversion of biomass (plant-derived material) to valuable fuels, chemicals, materials, and power, in order to reduce the United States' dependence on foreign oil; cut back on emissions that contribute to pollution; and encourage the growth of biorefineries, which provides jobs for many people.

Biomass is one of the United States' most important resources. It has been the largest U.S. renewable energy source since 2000. It also provides the only renewable alternative for liquid transportation fuel.

(a) This image shows the internals of a gas production module that converts wood chips into producer gas. (b) An ethanol powered snowplow in Hennepin County, Minnesota. *(a, courtesy National Renewable Energy Laboratory, photo by Jim Yost; b, courtesy of U.S. Department of Energy)*

Today's biomass uses include ethanol, biodiesel, biomass power, and industrial process energy.

In the future, biorefineries will use advanced technological processes such as hydrolysis of cellulosic biomass to sugars and lignin, and thermochemical conversion of biomass to synthesis gas for fermentation and catalysis of these platform chemicals to produce biopolymers and fuels. In order to expand the role of biomass in America's future, the Department of Energy's Biomass Program helps biomass technologies to advance as a result of their extensive and ongoing research and development.

The main goal of the federal government's energy program is to increase the nation's energy supplies using a more diverse mix of domestic resources. It also works to create a new bioindustry and reduce U.S. dependence on foreign oil by supplementing the use of petroleum for fuels and chemicals. According to the U.S. Department of Energy, in 2002, nonrenewable fossil fuels supplied 86% of the energy consumed in the United States. The United States imports more than half of its petroleum, and its dependency is increasing.

Declining U.S. oil reserves and falling domestic production from aging oil fields are key factors in America's increasing dependence on foreign imports. In addition, America has already developed the bulk of its known and easily accessible low-cost deposits. Today, four major producers provide the United States with oil—Canada, Mexico, Venezuela, and the Persian Gulf region (Bahrain, Iran, Iraq, Kuwait, Qatar, Saudi Arabia, and the United Arab Emirates).

Since the U.S. economy is so closely tied with petroleum products and oil imports, small changes in oil prices or disruptions in oil supplies can have an enormous impact on the economy—from trade deficits to industrial investment to employment levels, as has been seen over the past few years due to the current international political arena. The United States first experienced oil supply disruptions from the Persian Gulf region in the 1970s, when two sudden and sharp oil price hikes hit the American economy. Since then, additional disruptions in oil supplies, such as those occurring during the 1979 Iranian revolution, the 1990 invasion of Kuwait by Iraq, and the 2001 stand against international terrorism, reinforce the need to reduce America's dependence on Middle-Eastern oil. The ability of the United States to offset a major oil supply disruption has not improved much since the 1970s. As a domestic, renewable energy resource, biomass offers an alternative to conventional energy sources and provides national energy security, economic growth, and environmental benefits.

Agriculture and forestry residues—especially residues from paper mills—are the most common biomass resources used for generating electricity, industrial process heat, and steam for a variety of bio-based products. Current biomass consumption in the United States is dominated by industrial use—most of this energy is generated from wood. Use of liquid transportation fuels such as ethanol and biodiesel, however, currently derived from agricultural crops, is increasing dramatically. Ethanol and biodiesel, made from plant matter instead of petroleum, can be blended with or directly substituted for gasoline and diesel.

The use of biofuels is a good energy management endeavor because biofuels reduce toxic air emissions, greenhouse gas buildup, and dependence on imported oil, while supporting agriculture and America's rural communities. Unlike gasoline and diesel, biofuels contain oxygen. Adding biofuels to petroleum products allows the fuel to combust more completely, which reduces air pollution (much of the existing pollution is derived from inadequate burning of petroleum during the generation of power). In the future, as biomass energy gains momentum, "dedicated" **energy crops** may be grown—such as fast-growing trees and grasses—to supply the biomass.

THE BUILDING TECHNOLOGIES PROGRAM

The Department of Energy's current Building Technologies Program focuses on analyzing the components inside different types of buildings and determining the most efficient forms of the major features that compose them. For example, the program looks at building types, such as homes, multifamily dwellings (apartments), offices, retail stores, health-care facilities, hotels, schools, government buildings, and laboratories. The elements inside the building that the program researches in order to find the most energy-efficient options include appliances, ducts, heating and cooling, insulation, lighting, solar, water and water heating, and windows. The program also develops energy-efficient strategies to use when doing a remodel of an existing building. For those that rent living space, it provides energy-saving tips for responsible energy management, making it a program that everyone can benefit from.

The program advises thousands of homeowners on the many ways to save energy through the use of a programmable thermostat to control the heating and cooling of a home; how an individual can compare their energy use against the national average; how to conduct a home energy audit to determine the largest saving potential; how to install energy-efficient lighting, such as compact fluorescent lamps; and how to hire a professional to help homeowners insulate and repair the ducts in the house to keep costly energy from escaping. The Building Technologies Program is important because, according to the Department of Energy, the typical U.S. family spends more than $1,000 a year on home energy bills, and some of that energy is wasted, because heating, ventilating, and air-conditioning units are inefficient; windows leak conditioned air; and many appliances waste energy.

Not only is this energy inefficiency expensive, but it also harms the environment. For example, according to studies conducted by the federal government, electricity generated by fossil fuels for a single home puts more carbon dioxide into the air than two average cars.

New home construction presents an opportunity to incorporate energy-saving features right from the beginning. A major economic advantage is that energy-smart building choices save on energy bills. There are also many simple things people can do to better manage energy wisely, such as letting their clean dishes air-dry. Replacing standard light bulbs with fluorescents can save up to 50% on an average lighting energy bill. Replacing single-pane windows with double-pane windows and adding insulation also helps reduce heating and cooling costs.

In remodeling and new construction, many people are investing in solar panels to supply electricity and a solar water heater to provide hot

A hybrid car runs on a combination of gasoline and electric power. *(Photo by Nature's Images)*

water. Another option outlined in the federal government's Building Technologies Program is the use of ground source heat pumps that use the natural heat from the Earth to moderate the air temperature in the home.

FREEDOMCAR AND VEHICLE TECHNOLOGIES PROGRAM

The Department of Energy's FreedomCAR and Vehicle Technologies Program is developing more energy efficient and environmentally friendly highway transportation technologies that will enable Americans to use less petroleum. The goal of the program is to develop emission- and petroleum-free cars and light trucks. The program is conducting the research necessary to develop new technologies, such as fuel cells and advanced hybrid propulsion systems. By managing energy resources in this way, society will be able to cost-effectively move larger volumes of freight and greater numbers of passengers while emitting little or no pollution, with a dramatic reduction in dependence on imported oil.

The program's hybrid and vehicle systems research is done with industry partners. Automobile manufacturers and scientists from the program work together to design and test cutting-edge technologies.

Energy storage technologies, especially batteries, are also part of the program. Batteries are critical technologies for the development of advanced, fuel-efficient, light- and heavy-duty vehicles. They are currently in the process of developing durable and affordable batteries that cover many applications in a car's design, from start/stop to full-power electric, hybrid electric, and fuel cell vehicles. New batteries are being developed to be affordable, perform well, and be durable so that they can be used by many people.

Advanced internal combustion engines are also being developed to be more efficient in light-, medium-, and heavy-duty vehicles. Along with efficiency in mind, they are also being developed to meet future federal and state emissions regulations—an important component of pollution control. Scientists believe this technology will lead to an overall improvement of the energy efficiency of vehicles. Advanced internal combustion engines may also serve as an important element in the transition to hydrogen fuel cells.

New fuel types and lubricants are also being developed as part of the energy management program. The program's goal is to identify advanced petroleum- and non-petroleum-based fuels and lubricants for more energy-efficient and environmentally friendly highway transportation vehicles. Non-petroleum fuel components will come from non-fossil sources, such as biomass, vegetable oils, and waste animal fats.

Research into materials technologies is another important component of the program. According to recent studies by the Department of Energy, advanced materials, including metals, polymers, composites, and intermetallic compounds, can play an important role in improving the efficiency of transportation engines and vehicles. Weight reduction is one of the most practical ways to improve fuel efficiency. The use of lightweight, high-performance materials are expected to contribute to the development of vehicles that provide better fuel economy, but are still comparable in size, comfort, and safety to today's vehicles.

GEOTHERMAL TECHNOLOGIES PROGRAM

The Department of Energy's Geothermal Technologies Program works as a partner with industries to establish geothermal energy as an economically competitive contributor to the United States' energy supply. The Department of Energy works with individual power companies; industrial and residential consumers; and federal, state, and local officials to provide technical, industrial support, and cost-shared funding. The federal government even offers tax credits to businesses that use geothermal energy. Geothermal power is most commonly found in the western portions of the United States.

SOLAR ENERGY TECHNOLOGIES PROGRAM

The federal government's Solar Technologies Program is designed to develop solar energy technologies that supply clean, renewable power to the United States. This program focuses on five different types of energy management:

- Low-grade thermal energy for heating homes and businesses
- Medium-grade thermal energy for industrial processes
- High-grade thermal energy for driving turbines to generate electricity
- Electrical energy, converted directly from sunlight, to provide electricity for homes and other buildings
- Chemical energy in hydrogen for use in fuel cells and many electrical, heating, and transportation applications

Like other clean, renewable energy sources, solar energy technologies have great potential to benefit the nation. They can diversify our energy supply, reduce the dependence on imported fuels, improve air quality, lower the amount of greenhouse gases generated from other energy sources, and provide jobs for many people.

Heat energy created from the sun's energy can be used to generate electricity in a steam generator. Because solar energy is fairly inexpensive and has the ability to provide power when and where it is needed, it can be a major contributor to the nation's future needs for energy.

An exciting new development in solar technology is hybrid solar lighting, which collects sunlight and routes it through optical fibers into buildings where it is combined with electric light in "hybrid" light fixtures. Automatic sensors keep the room at a steady lighting level by adjusting the electric lights based on the sunlight currently available. This new generation of solar lighting combines both electric and solar power.

GOVERNMENT MANAGEMENT ON PUBLIC LANDS FOR MULTIPLE USES

The federal and state governments manage millions of acres of public lands across the country. These different lands can have many designated uses. For example, they can be used for mineral acquisition and the mining of oil, gas, coal, oil shale, tar sands, and uranium. They can be used for commercial purposes such as ranching, grazing, farming, and logging. They can be used for recreation—hiking, backpacking, off-road-vehicle touring, boating, camping, hunting, horseback riding, and bird watching. The same land also fits within an ecosystem, home to thousands of species of plants and animals.

Managers of the land sometimes have to make difficult decisions on what types of activities should be permitted. Sometimes, different uses—although each use may be compatible with the land—conflict with each other. For example, mineable oil, gas, and minerals may be found in the same places as endangered wildlife habitat, fragile ecosystems, and rare and exotic plant species. In the western United States where many geologic basins exist that contain oil and gas resources, there is also sage-grouse habitat—a bird species that has earned the attention from biologists and ecologists over the past few years as the species habitat has been endangered, negatively impacted, and populations of the bird have significantly dwindled. In this case, energy development on the land can cause severe problems, even if oil and gas resources are present.

In other areas, wind machines can be put in areas where livestock graze without having a negative impact. Responsible multiple use of the land is the goal of the federal government. It is these issues that land managers must constantly address so that all natural resources are managed properly.

OIL SPILLS AND ENVIRONMENTAL IMPACTS

Refineries today are making cleaner fuels and also making them differently, emitting less and recycling more of the chemicals used in the refining process. Through safety guidelines currently in place, oil spills occur less often. Underground storage tanks and piping are checked regularly for leaks. Special equipment keeps gasoline vapors from entering the air when fuel is transferred from one tank to another. Service stations collect used oil from motorists for recycling and reuse. These practices all represent sound management techniques.

Occasionally, however, there are problems with petroleum that result from its use. In transporting oil, accidents do happen. Oil spills can kill plants and animals and contaminate beaches. Spills may also happen closer to home—people often dump used oil from vehicle engines onto the ground or into open drains instead of taking it to a certified recycling center. This causes pollution. Plastic objects and containers are thrown away, but the plastic does not decay quickly. It stays around and can injure or kill wildlife. For example, the plastic holders commonly used to bundle soft drink six-packs have strangled birds and other wildlife. Plastic bags discarded in the oceans have killed sea turtles that mistook them for a jellyfish or other food source.

Commercial oil spills are especially destructive to the environment. Oil spills into rivers, bays, and the ocean are caused by accidents involving tankers, barges, pipelines, refineries, and storage facilities, usually while the oil is being transported to the users. Spills can be caused by people making mistakes or being careless, equipment breaking down, natural disasters such as hurricanes, deliberate acts by terrorists, countries at war, vandals, or illegal dumpers.

When a spill happens, the oil floats on the surface of the ocean. The oil then spreads out rapidly across the surface into a thin layer called an oil slick. As it continues to spread, the layer thins even more into a sheen, which sometimes looks like a rainbow (similar to sheens in parking lots after a rain).

The Exxon Valdez Oil Spill and Its Long-term Impacts

On March 24, 1989, the *Exxon Valdez* grounded on Bligh Reef, and spilled nearly 11 million gallons (42 million L) of oil into the biologically rich waters of Prince William Sound in Alaska. This was the largest oil spill in the United States. Even though a major cleanup was enacted, over 15 years later, oil still persists in certain environments, especially in areas sheltered from weathering processes, such as the subsurface under selected gravel shorelines, and in some soft substrates containing peat.

The *Exxon Valdez* spill served to make the American public aware of environmental health in a new way. The images of heavily oiled shorelines, dead and dying wildlife, and the thousands of workers mobilized to clean beaches reflect what many people felt was the ultimate environmental insult in a previously pristine and biologically rich area. Since the spill, both scientists and the public alike have shown concern for the health of the environment and human impacts on fragile ecosystems.

Surface oil today has all but disappeared. Where it is still found is in areas beneath the surface and where oil initially penetrated very deeply and was not removed. It is still difficult today for scientists to completely assess the impacts from the disturbance because the ecosystem is so fragile and dynamic. One positive point, however, is that since the spill, scientists have learned from misfortune and now more fully understand how oil spills should be responded to, how they should be cleaned up, and how to best enable an area to recover.

(a) Submerged oil, such as this spill off the coast of Florida, can cause severe habitat problems and environmental damage. (b) Sea otters are often adversely affected by oil spills. When oil saturates their fur, they lose their ability to stay warm in the cold water. Ingestion of too much oil while trying to clean their fur can lead to death. *(a, courtesy of U.S. Fish and Wildlife Service, Florida Environmental Protection Agency; b, courtesy National Oceanic and Atmospheric Administration)*

Oil spills can be very harmful to marine birds and mammals, and can also harm fish and shellfish. Oil destroys the insulating ability of fur-bearing animals, such as sea otters, and the water-repelling abilities of a bird's feathers, exposing these animals to the harsh environmental elements (cold water, cold air, and strong winds).

Many birds and mammals also ingest (swallow) oil when they try to clean themselves, which can poison them. Sometimes, thousands of birds and mammals die as a result of oil spills.

Once a spill happens, local, state, and federal government agencies as well as volunteer organizations respond to the incident. The method used for cleanup depends on the specific circumstances of the spill. (For example, road equipment works on sand and beaches, but not in marshes or areas with large boulders.) Sometimes stations are set up where they can clean and rehabilitate wildlife. Sometimes, no response is made because it may cause more harm and damage than help. In the United States, depending on where the spill occurs, either the U.S. Coast Guard or the U.S. Environmental Protection Agency (EPA) takes charge of the spill response.

When an oil spill is responded to, several types of countermeasures can be made to reduce the harm of the spill. One method is through the use of dispersants. These are chemicals that are applied directly to the spilled oil in order to remove it from the water surface, where oil can be especially harmful. Planes flying over the surface of the water drop the dispersant onto the surface. After several weeks, dispersed oil droplets degrade into naturally occurring substances. Dispersants work better when the ocean has moderate waves. It is difficult to disperse oil in water with high waves or a flat, calm sea.

It is important to have a routine energy management plan in place for the use of any type of energy, based on current technology. It is also important—as in the case of an oil spill—to have an emergency plan in place.

CHAPTER 8

CONSERVATION OF ENERGY RESOURCES

The previous chapters have illustrated the various types of energy resources found on Earth and their contributions to the lives of humans. This chapter examines the conservation of these precious resources. It begins by looking at energy efficiency and conservation and then solid waste conservation and transportation conservation. Next, it presents energy-saving tips for homeowners and what elements of homes can save the most energy. In conclusion, it looks at reducing, reusing, and recycling and what everyone can do to conserve precious energy resources.

ENERGY EFFICIENCY AND CONSERVATION

The United States uses a lot of energy—nearly a million dollars' worth each minute, 24 hours a day, every day of the year. With less than 5% of the world's population, Americans consume about one-fourth of the world's energy resources. According to the U.S. Department of Energy, the average American consumes six times more energy than the world average. The table on page 152 illustrates the energy usage of various countries.

In order to maintain our quality of life, however, energy resources must be used wisely. The choices we make about how energy is used—such as turning machines off when they are not being used or choosing to buy energy-efficient appliances—impact the environment and our lives. There are many conservation methods that allow less energy to be used more wisely. These things involve energy efficiency and conservation.

Representative Countries and Energy Usage

Country	Population in millions	Energy consumption in quadrillion Btus
China	1,295	43.2
India	1,050	14.0
United States	288	97.4
Brazil	176	8.6
Pakistan	150	1.8
Russia	144	27.5
Bangladesh	144	0.6
Japan	128	22.0
Nigeria	121	0.9
Mexico	102	6.6
Germany	82	14.3
France	60	11.0
United Kingdom	59	9.6
Italy	57	7.6
South Korea	47	8.4
Canada	31	13.1

Source: U.S. Department of Energy

Energy conservation practices result in the use of less energy. Energy efficiency involves the use of technology that requires less energy to perform the same function. For example, a compact fluorescent lightbulb that uses less energy than an incandescent bulb to produce the same amount of light is an example of energy efficiency. The actual decision to replace an incandescent light bulb with a compact fluorescent is an example of energy conservation.

The U.S. Department of Energy divides the way people use energy into four categories—residential, commercial, industrial, and transportation. Each person has the ability to make energy choices and take actions that can result in the reduction in the amount of energy used in all sectors of the economy.

According to the U.S. Department of Energy, households use about one-fifth of the total energy consumed in the United States each year. The typical U.S. family spends about $1,500 a year on utility bills. About 60% is in the form of electricity; the remainder comes mostly from natural gas and oil.

A great deal of this energy is not put to use. Heat pours out of homes through drafty doors and windows, and through ceilings and walls that are not insulated. Some appliances use energy 24 hours a day, even when they are turned off.

Energy-efficient improvements can make a home more comfortable and save money. Many utility companies throughout the country provide energy audits to identify areas where homes are wasting energy. In this chapter, the reader will see how making small changes in a home—such as adding insulation, putting in double-pane windows, and changing traditional lightbulbs to fluorescent bulbs—can drastically change the efficiency of a home.

There are many components found in an energy-efficient house. The federal government's Energy Star program independently qualifies many homes as energy efficient—meaning they are in the top 25% of energy-efficient homes. Things such as tight construction, high performance windows, controlled air infiltration, improved insulation, upgraded heating and cooling systems, tight duct systems, and upgraded water-heating equipment can be verified by the government and classed as an Energy Star home. Energy Star homes save money, allow equipment to last longer, are often more safe, and raise the value of the house.

People who live in multifamily dwellings—such as apartments and condominiums—can also practice conservation in order to reduce

What You Can Do to Save Energy

It is important to save energy because most of the energy we use comes from nonrenewable fossil fuels. It would be impossible to stop using energy, but there are many things everyone can do to save energy, such as the following:

- Wear a sweatshirt or other warm clothing indoors when it is cold, so the furnace does not have to be set as high.
- Turn off all the lights when leaving a room.
- Replace standard lightbulbs with fluorescent lightbulbs.
- Turn off the television, radio, and computer when they are not being used.
- Ride the bus to school.
- Reduce, reuse, and recycle.
- Buy products without packaging and wrapping.
- Recycle newspapers. Paper made from recycled paper uses about one-third less energy than paper made from raw materials.
- Recycle glass bottles and jars. Glass products made from recycled glass use about one-third less energy than those made from raw materials.
- Recycle steel and aluminum cans. Aluminum cans made from recycled aluminum use 90% less energy than aluminum made from raw materials.
- Buy products made of recycled material. Look for the "recycle" mark (three arrows that make a circle) on the package.

power bills. During the cold months, when the residence is occupied, the thermostat should be set between 65°F and 85°F (18°C and 20°C). When no one is home, the thermostat should be set to 50°F to 55°F (10°C to 13°C). Conversely, in the warmer months, do not set the air conditioner below 78°F (25.6°C). Natural sunlight—instead of electric lighting—should be used whenever possible. Also, lamps should be positioned to make the most of their light.

Another way to conserve energy is by leaving seldom-used appliances—such as extra color televisions, computers, radios, stereos, and VCRs—unplugged when not in use, because they draw as much as 10 watts (7 kWh/month) even when they are not turned on. It is also important to keep appliances in good working order. When baking in the oven, do not open the oven door any more than absolutely necessary, because the oven loses about 20% of its heat every time the door is opened.

Only run full loads in the dishwasher. Use the air-dry (or energy saver) option, if available. The hot water temperature should be checked at the faucet with a **thermometer**. The temperature at the hot water heater should be adjusted so that the faucet temperature is 120°F (49°C).

Home-automation systems can also be used to conserve energy. There are currently three types of home automation controls: individual control devices, distributed control devices, and centrally controlled systems.

Individual devices control only one appliance. These are things like programmable thermostats, motion detectors, photo lighting controls, and timers. An example is a television remote control unit.

A distributed-control system uses standard power line wiring, telephone wire, video wire, radio signals, or infrared signals. Microchip controls must be installed in the appliances or outlets. This system allows individual appliances to communicate with each other over existing electrical wiring. A TV set can be used to monitor the system's status.

The positive thing about having a centrally-controlled system is that everything is linked together and controlled from one location.

The central computer can control "dumb" appliances—those that do not have individual microprocessor chips that allow them to interact with the configuration, as well as "smart" appliances that do have those capabilities. Smart appliances are also able to communicate potential problems, such as a short circuit or incompatibility. When a signal of a potential problem with an appliance is detected by the central computer, the power is cut to that appliance, thereby preventing an accident from occurring.

Natural gas management can also be controlled in this way. Gas outlets can be installed throughout a home. The "smart" gas outlets constantly monitor for leaks, bad connections, or any other problem, and shut off gas to the outlet if it is unsafe. One of the best features about this system is that if smoke were detected, it would automatically shut off the flow of gas from the main valve to prevent a fire or an explosion—an important safety issue in any household.

Sophisticated home automation systems are still in their infancy and are expensive. Except for low-end security systems with some lighting and climate control added, they are currently targeted at the new luxury home market. Future developments of home automation will be explored in Chapter 9.

SOLID WASTE CONSERVATION

Garbage, or Municipal Solid Waste (MSW), and deciding what to do with it is not a new problem—it has existed for centuries. As America's population has grown, the amount of waste has increased dramatically. Today, about 55% of our garbage is buried in landfills. Americans produce more waste each year. According to the Office of the Federal Environment Executive, over the past 30 years, the waste produced in this country has more than doubled—from 88 million tons in 1960 to 232 million tons in 2002.

Lifestyles have changed, too. People are buying more convenience items and more disposables. Today, the average American generates 4.4 pounds of trash every day. Most experts agree that MSW should be handled in four progressive steps:

1. Source reduction: Reducing the amount of waste produced
    in the first place. For example, using less aluminum to
    make an aluminum can or glass to make a bottle.
2. Recycling: Using old products to make new products—
    such as using old newspapers to make egg cartons or
    recycled paper to produce newspaper.
3. Waste to energy: Burning trash to produce steam and
    electricity.
4. Landfilling: Bury waste when it cannot, or should not, be
    burned or recycled.

Given the fast-paced lifestyle of modern families and the current
quality of life, Americans are unlikely to give up the comfort and convenience of disposable products. Common sense tells us that reducing
the amount of waste we produce is the easiest way to solve America's
growing garbage problem. Reducing waste at the beginning conserves
energy and natural resources.

Packaging—the way the product is wrapped or boxed—has become
the target of most source reduction efforts. Packaging is the single largest product in the waste stream and includes boxes, plastics, Styrofoam,
paper wrappers, cardboard, and containers.

Packaging provides a convenient and sanitary way to store and
transport food and other products; but sometimes the packaging is
just a marketing gimmick to make a product look more attractive. For
example, many toys are placed in colorful boxes and individual containers so that their increased aesthetic appeal will get a consumer's
attention, making them more likely to buy it. In fact, about 10% of the
cost of merchandise goes toward the packaging. By weight, packaging
makes up one-third of MSW.

Environmentally oriented manufacturers today are trying to solve
this problem—they are redesigning products so they need less packaging and are using fewer materials to package products. For example,
the soft drink industry is making thinner bottles and cans; disposable
diapers are thinner than before; and even the fast-food restaurant

McDonald's has made its drinking straws lighter in order to eliminate 1 million pounds (454 thousand kg) of solid waste per year.

Recycling can save energy. It almost always takes less energy to make a product from recycled materials than it does to make it from new materials. Many different commodities are recycled, such as plastic containers, glass containers, yard waste, trees, paper and paperboard, aluminum packaging, steel cans, and auto batteries. One type of recycling is called "closed loop" recycling. It is making an old product into the same thing again. For example, turning an old glass jar into a new glass jar, or turning old newspaper back into new newspaper. Closed loop recycling is ideal because there is already an existing market for the recycled product.

Another solution to controlling the amount of garbage that collects is to burn it. All organic waste contains energy. Organic waste is that made from plant or animal products. Wood is one type of organic material that has been burned for years. Coal is another organic material that is burned for energy.

Garbage can be burned in special plants and its energy used to make steam to heat buildings or to generate electricity. Garbage does not contain as much heat as coal. It takes one ton (2,000 pounds or 907 kg) of garbage to equal the heat energy in 500 pounds (227 kg) of coal. Today there are 103 waste-to-energy plants in the United States.

Biodegradation

Biodegradation is a natural process that happens when microorganisms—such as bacteria or fungi—secrete enzymes that chemically break down or degrade dead plants and animals. Biodegradation is when waste decays or rots.

Most organic wastes are biodegradable under normal environmental conditions. Given enough time, the waste will disintegrate into harmless substances, therefore enriching the soil with nutrients.

The United States burns 15% of its solid waste—14% in waste-to-energy plants and 1% in old-style incinerators.

The federal government has determined that waste-to-energy plants generate enough electricity to supply 2.4 million households; but generating electricity is not the advantage of burning garbage—it is actually more expensive to generate electricity from garbage than it is to use a coal, nuclear, or hydropower plant. Instead, the major advantage of burning waste is that it reduces the amount of garbage that is buried in landfills. Waste-to-energy plants dispose of the waste of 40 million people.

Landfills are where the majority—55%—of garbage ends up, hauled off in garbage trucks every day and dumped into sanitary landfills. There will always be a need for landfills—even if some garbage is recycled or burned—because not all waste can be recycled or burned. Landfill burial is the only feasible way to dispose of some types of waste, and sometimes it is the safest method. Usually, landfills are the best disposal method for hazardous wastes—batteries, paints, and pesticides. Landfills are also designed to prevent hazardous wastes from seeping into underground water supplies. Therefore, developing landfills takes special well-thought-out planning.

When a landfill is full, it is sealed and covered with a final cap of impermeable clay and dirt. Ground wells in the area are monitored for years afterward in order to document the quality of groundwater on and around the site to ensure environmentally sound conditions.

TRANSPORTATION CONSERVATION

Based on studies conducted by the U.S. Department of Energy, transportation accounts for more than 67% of the oil consumed in the United States. The United States imports more than 54% of its oil supply. It is estimated that by 2010, the import rate will have risen to 75%.

The U.S. Federal Highway Administration has determined that the average vehicle on the road today emits more than 600 pounds (272 kg) of air pollution each year. The pollution—carbon monoxide, sulfur dioxide, nitrogen dioxide, and particulate matter—unfortunately contributes to smog and health problems for many people.

The increased use of fossil fuels during the last century has created and enhanced the greenhouse effect—also known as global warming. Alternate fuel vehicles (AFVs) and advanced vehicle technologies help combat both air pollution and global climate change.

Alternative fuels not only burn cleaner—producing lower emissions—but some are even renewable (unlike fossil fuels), which means a continuous supply could be developed. The alternative fuels in use today include ethanol, biodiesel, methanol, natural gas, propane, electricity, and hydrogen. Characteristics of these fuels have been discussed in previous chapters.

The P-series is a relatively new alternative fuel. It is a blend of ethanol, methyltetrahydrofuran (MTHF), and pentanes, with butane added for blends used in severe cold weather. The Environmental Protection Agency has determined that emissions from producing and using P-series are much less than those from gasoline. P-series was initially developed as a fuel to help fleets meet the U.S. Energy Policy Act's requirement to purchase more AFVs. Eventually, they will be available to the general public, as well.

Today, there are three basic types of AFVs: flex-fuel, bifuel or dual-fuel, and dedicated vehicles. A flex-fuel vehicle (FFV) has one tank and can accept any mixture of gasoline and either methanol or ethanol. According to the U.S. Department of Energy, there are already one to two million FFVs on America's roads today.

Bifuel vehicles have two tanks—one for gasoline and one for either natural gas or propane, depending on the vehicle. The vehicles can switch between the two fuels. Dedicated vehicles are designed to be fueled only by one alternative fuel.

Some cars on the market now offer considerable improvements in fuel economy. Other advanced technologies are under development and will soon be available in new vehicles.

Hybrid electric vehicles (HEVs) are also becoming more common on the road. These cars get roughly twice the mileage to the gallon as conventional vehicles.

Advanced technologies have even been developed on the vehicle's engines. For example, the compression-ignition, direct-injection (CIDI) engines are the most efficient internal combustion engines available today. They can directly inject fuel into the combustion chamber of an engine to ignite the fuel by compressing it. Turbocharged direct-injection (TDI) diesel engines get 20% better mileage than conventional diesel engines.

The fuel cell is one of the most attractive advanced vehicle technologies today. Many researchers expect this technology to be used in vehicles by 2010. Fuel cells, which convert hydrogen and oxygen into electricity, have been researched for use in vehicles for many years, and because of it, their development and performance have progressed. Because they produce only water vapor as emissions, fuel cells promise to be ideal power sources for transportation. They can be used as the main power for an electric vehicle, or in conjunction with an internal combustion engine in a hybrid vehicle. Fuel cells convert the chemical energy of a fuel into usable electricity and heat without combustion as an intermediate step. Fuel cells are similar to batteries in that they produce a direct current by means of an electrochemical process. Today, researchers are working on making fuel cell components of a size, weight, and cost that is competitive with internal combustion engines.

Mass transportation provides another convenient way to conserve energy. Many modes of mass transit today use innovative and advanced technology designed to be energy efficient.

Solar-powered vehicles (SPVs), such as cars, boats, bicycles, and even airplanes, use solar energy to either power an electric motor directly and/or use solar energy to charge a battery which powers the motor. They use an array of solar photovoltaic (PV) cells that convert sunlight into electricity. The electricity either goes directly to an electric motor powering the vehicle or to a storage battery. The PV array can be built onto the vehicle body itself or fixed on a building or a vehicle shelter to charge an electric vehicle (EV) battery when it is parked. Other types of renewable energy sources—such as wind energy or hydropower—can also produce electricity cleanly to charge EV batteries.

Riding efficient public transportation is another way to conserve energy resources. (a) An electric light rail train. (b) A bus powered by natural gas. (c) A hybrid-electric bus. *(a, b, photos by Nature's Images; c, photo by Utah Transit Authority, photo by Andrea Knopp and Leslie Fiet)*

Ed Passerini built the first totally solar-power car—called the "Bluebird" in 1977. Since then, major automobile manufacturers—such as General Motors, Ford, and Honda—have begun developing solar cars with advanced technology.

Solar car races are becoming increasingly popular events in the United States. The first American Solar Cup was held in 1988 in Visalia,

The American Solar Challenge, the longest solar car race in the world, is a U.S. Department of Energy sponsored educational event in which teams compete to build and race solar-powered cars. The race starts in Chicago, Illinois, and stretches 2,300 miles (3,701 km) to Claremont, California. *(Courtesy U.S. Department of Energy)*

California. The Sunrayce was first run in 1990 from Florida's Epcot Center to Warren, Michigan. The first American Solar Challenge, sponsored by the U.S. Department of Energy, the National Renewable Energy Laboratory, and Terion Inc., was held in 2001, covering 2,300 miles (3,700 km) from Chicago, Illinois, to Claremont, California. Other popular solar race events that are held include solar bike races and solar boat races.

ENERGY SAVERS AND CONSERVATION TIPS FOR HOMES

Energy-efficient improvements can make a home more comfortable and save money. Changes can be made to heating and cooling methods, insulation and weatherization, doors and windows, landscaping, electricity and appliances, lighting, and methods of water heating.

Heating and Cooling

Heating and cooling systems use more energy than any other systems in homes. Typically, 42% of an average family's energy bills are spent to keep homes at a comfortable temperature. Simply adjusting the thermostat by two degrees (lower in winter, higher in summer) can lower heating bills by 4% and prevent 500 pounds (227 kg) of carbon dioxide from entering the atmosphere each year. Programmable thermostats can automatically control temperature for the time of day and the season.

In the summer, homes can also be cooled naturally. Depending on the geographic location, keeping cool indoors when it is hot outdoors can be a challenge. The sunlight beating down on a home causes the indoor temperature to become too hot. Without using air-conditioning, the most effective method to cool the home is to keep the heat from building up in the first place. The primary source of heat buildup is sunlight absorbed through the roof, walls, and windows. Secondary sources are heat-generating appliances in the home and air leakage. Heat can be reflected away from the roof by applying a reflective coating to the existing roof or installing a radiant barrier on the underside of the roof. A radiant barrier is just a sheet of aluminum foil with a paper backing. It has been shown that radiant barriers can reduce heat gain by 25%. Also, the lighter in color the exterior walls of the house are, the more heat they will reflect away from the house.

Geothermal heat pumps (GHPs) are another alternative to heating and cooling buildings. GHPs are also known as ground-source or water-source heat pumps, and are available for both commercial and residential buildings. They can be installed anywhere throughout the United States and are the most energy-efficient, environmentally clean, and cost-effective space conditioning systems available today. They are also very quiet and offer free or reduced-cost hot water. GHPs use the Earth as a heat sink in the summer and a heat source in the winter—they rely on the relative natural warmth of the Earth for their heating and cooling production. Through a system of underground or underwater pipes, they transfer heat from the Earth or water source to the building in the winter, and take the heat from the building in the summer and discharge it into the cooler ground.

Therefore, the GHP takes heat from a warm area and exchanges the heat to a cooler area, and vice versa. Because it can be used for both heating and cooling, it eliminates the need for separate furnace and air conditioning systems—another environmental and economic advantage. GHPs use 25%–50% less electricity than conventional heating and cooling systems.

Solar collectors can also be used to produce heat by trapping the Sun's rays. Most solar collectors are boxes, frames, or rooms that contain the following parts:

- Clear covers that allow solar energy to enter.
- Dark surfaces inside, called absorber plates, which soak up heat.
- Insulation materials to prevent the heat from escaping.
- Vents or pipes that carry the heated air or liquid from inside the collector to where it can be utilized.

Glass is the most common material used for covers. When sunlight passes through glass and hits a surface inside a solar collector, it changes into heat. The glass is very efficient at trapping the heat produced inside the collector.

The heat produced in the collector is then soaked up, or absorbed, by metal sheets or containers filled with water or rocks that have been painted black. Adequate insulation prevents, or slows down, the movement of heat. Vents or fans then carry the heated air from the collector to other parts of the house, effectively warming it.

Another available method of heating rooms is by radiant floor heating. Radiant floor heating is a heating technique that has been around for centuries. These heating systems use channels or pipes that are embedded in, or installed under, the floor. Floors made of concrete or some other dense material hold heat the best. A heated fluid (air, water, or other heat transfer fluid) is blown or pumped through this network.

The thermal mass of the floor absorbs the heat from the fluid and radiates it evenly into the living space. The thermal mass of the floor acts as a heat battery, making these systems very efficient. Radiant floor heating systems also allow the heating appliance to fire at a slower rate and less often, saving fuel.

During the last few decades, radiant floor heating systems have been adapted to use solar energy. In many areas of the country, there is not enough solar energy available to heat a house by itself, but it can supplement a conventional furnace or boiler. This could reduce heating fuel consumption from 10%–90%.

Although many people use fireplaces part of the year to heat their homes, wood-burning fireplaces may actually remove more heat from a house than they produce. In fact, a typical vertical-back fireplace with an open front is only about 10% efficient in converting wood to energy and delivering it to a room. The rest of the heat goes up through the chimney and outdoors. In addition, these fireplaces pull cold air into the house from small gaps around windows and doors.

In order to have an efficient fireplace, an insert must be installed. Fireplace inserts are wood-, pellet-, or gas-fueled appliances that fit into a conventional open fireplace. Most inserts have tight-fitting glass or metal doors and built-in air circulation features. The most efficient models supply combustion air from outside the house. Some inserts have fans to circulate air into the room. Fans improve the heat distribution by 50%–75%.

The type of home can also make a difference in how warm or cool a house stays. The type of landscaping also plays an important role. For example, log homes can be more energy efficient. Logs have a greater heat storage capacity compared to other traditional building materials. Logs act like "thermal batteries" and can, under the right circumstances, store heat during the day and gradually release it at night.

Earth-sheltered houses are another energy conservative design, although they are not common. These houses are built with the bulk of the house underground. Because these types of houses are thermally controlled by the Earth's natural heat, they are less susceptible to the impact

Specific designs of homes can encourage energy efficiency. (a) A log home has thick walls and can store heat during the day then release it slowly at night. (b) Providing ample landscaping around a home can protect from overheating from sunlight, thereby conserving energy. *(a, photo by Nature's Images; b, photo by National Renewable Energy Laboratory)*

of extreme outdoor air temperatures, so the effects of adverse weather are not as noticeable as those in a conventional house. Temperatures inside the house are more stable than a conventional house.

Overhangs on a building can also help conserve energy. Overhangs serve to shade windows, doors, and walls. In the Northern Hemisphere, they are most effective on areas that face south and all areas at midday. Overhangs usually only affect the amount of direct solar radiation that strikes a surface.

Insulation and Weatherization

Adding **insulation** and weatherization products can reduce heating and cooling needs. Warm air leaking into the home in the summer and out of the home in the winter can waste a significant amount of energy. Insulation is like wrapping a house in a thermal blanket. Unfortunately, if there are small cracks or leaks in the house to the outside, they have an effect comparable to keeping a door open. One of the easiest money-saving measures that can be done to the house is to caulk, seal, and weather-strip all the cracks to the outside. It is possible to save 10% or more on energy bills if a house is properly insulated and weatherized.

There are many types of insulation. Loose-fill insulations are usually composed of small pieces of cellulose, fiberglass, polyurethane foam, or rock wool. They are mixed with an adhesive and blown into building cavities using special equipment. The insulation fills up all the air pockets in a home that could let cold air inside. Loose-fill insulation is also environmentally friendly because recycled waste materials are used to make it. For example, cellulose insulation is made from wastepaper, such as newspaper and shredded boxes. Chemicals are added to provide resistance to fires and insects.

Other types of insulation come in batts, or rolls. These types are commonly used when building new houses because they can be installed without needing special equipment—the insulation is rolled out and attached to the walls before the walls are sealed off. Insulation can be put into walls, floors, attic spaces, and any other open cavities where air might escape. The more leaks that are sealed off, the warmer in winter (or cooler in summer) the house will stay. When new homes are built, the outside of the foundation can also be insulated with a rigid fiberglass mat.

The use of radiant barriers are another way to conserve energy. A radiant barrier is simply a reflective surface. A good example of a radiant barrier is aluminum cooking foil, since it reflects heat into or away from food while cooking. Just like aluminum foil, radiant barriers can keep unwanted heat out of buildings.

A single layer of reflective material, properly installed between the roof and the attic floor of a home, can reduce heat gain from the sun to the attic by about 95%. Radiant barriers are also very effective for walls that get direct sunlight hitting them.

Simple caulking and weather stripping can also increase the energy efficiency of a home. Caulk is a putty-like substance that can be put around water pipes, faucets, drains, windows, and doorframes. Weather stripping can seal leaks around movable joints, such as windows and doors. Warmed or air-conditioned air mixes with outside air through gaps in the home's thermal envelope—exterior walls, windows, doors, the roof, and floors. Air leaks like this can waste huge amounts of energy. Most experts agree that caulking and weather stripping any gaps will pay for itself within one year in energy savings. Caulking and weather stripping will also reduce drafts in the house and make it feel warmer when it is cold outside. Caulking and weather stripping are two techniques commonly done along with insulating.

Doors and Windows

About one-third of a typical home's heat loss occurs through the doors and windows. Energy-efficient doors are insulated and seal tightly to prevent air from leaking through or around them. Insulated storm doors provide an additional barrier to leaking air.

Most homes have more windows than doors. Replacing older windows with new energy-efficient ones can reduce both air leaks and utility bills. The best of these windows shut tightly and are constructed of two or more pieces of glass separated by a gas that does not conduct heat well.

It is also possible to make older windows more energy efficient. Caulking any cracks around the window frames so that they are sealed tightly can help. Adding storm windows or sheets of clear plastic to the outside to create additional air barriers can also help. Insulated drapes can be hung on the inside. During the winter, it is most functional to open them on sunny days and close them at night, thereby effectively letting heat into the home and keeping it there when it is colder outside. During the summer, it is best to close them during the day to keep out the heat from the sunlight.

Windows, doors, and skylights are currently part of the government-backed Energy Star program that certifies energy-efficient products.

In order to meet Energy Star requirements, windows, doors, and skylights must meet requirements tailored for the country's three broad climate regions.

Landscaping

Although it is not possible to control the weather, landscaping can help reduce its impact on home energy use. By placing trees, shrubs, and other landscape structures to block the wind and provide shade, people can reduce the energy needed to keep their homes comfortable during heating and cooling seasons.

Electricity and Appliances

Appliances account for about 20% of a typical household's energy use, with refrigerators, clothes washers, and dryers the most used. When shopping for new appliances, it is important to note the listed cost of operating the appliance during its lifetime. Many energy-efficient appliances cost more to buy, but save money in lower energy costs. Over the life of an appliance, an energy-efficient model is always a better deal. Energy-efficient appliances are labeled with the Energy Star certification. The U.S. Department of Energy has determined that by using these energy-efficient appliances, energy bills can be reduced by 30%.

Lighting

The people of the United States spend about one-quarter of electricity produced on lighting, at a cost of more than $37 billion each year. Much of this energy is wasted using inefficient incandescent lightbulbs. Only 10% of the energy used by an incandescent bulb produces light; the rest is given off as wasted heat. If 25% of the lightbulbs in a house are replaced with fluorescents, it can save about 50% on electricity bills. Compact fluorescent lightbulbs (CFLs) provide the same amount of light and no longer flicker or buzz. CFLs cost more to buy, but they save money in the long run because they use only one-quarter the energy of incandescent bulbs and last 8–12 times longer. According to the U.S.

Department of Energy, each CFL you install can save $30–$60 over the bulb's life.

Water Heating

Water heating is the third largest energy expense in the home. It typically accounts for about 14% of the utility bill. Heated water is used for many applications, such as showers, baths, laundry, dishwashing, and general cleaning. There are four ways to cut water-heating bills—use less hot water; turn down the thermostat on the water heater; insulate the water heater and pipes; and buy a new, more efficient water heater. Other ways to conserve hot water include taking showers instead of baths, taking shorter showers, fixing leaks in faucets and pipes, and using the lowest temperature wash and rinse settings on clothes washers.

Manufacturing

Manufacturing the goods that are used every day consumes an enormous amount of energy. The industrial sector of the U.S. economy consumes one-third of the energy used in the United States.

In the industrial sector, the market drives energy efficiency and conservation measures. Manufacturers know that they must keep their costs low to compete in the global economy. Since energy is one of the biggest costs in many industries, manufacturers must use energy-efficient technologies and conservation measures in order to be successful. According to the National Renewable Energy Laboratory, manufacturer's demand for energy-efficient equipment drives much of the research and development of new technologies. Individual consumers can, however, have an effect on industrial energy use through the product choices they make and what they do with packaging and products they no longer use.

REDUCE, REUSE, AND RECYCLE

Every American throws away about 1,000 pounds (454 kg) of trash a year. The most effective way for consumers to help reduce the amount of energy consumed by industry is to decrease the number of unnecessary products produced and to reuse items wherever possible. Purchasing only items that are necessary, and reusing and recycling products can reduce energy use in the industrial sector.

Fortunately, everyone can take an active role in reducing, reusing, and recycling materials. According to the U.S. Environmental Protection Agency, in order to reduce consumption, each person should buy only what they need. Purchasing fewer goods means less to throw away. It also results in fewer goods being produced and less energy being used in the manufacturing process. Buying goods with less packaging also reduces the amount of waste generated and the amount of energy used.

Products should be bought that can be used multiple times. If items are bought that can be reused, rather than disposable items that are used once and thrown away, it will save natural resources. It will also save the energy used to make them, and reduce the amount of landfill space needed to contain the waste after they are used.

In order to make a significant difference on the environment, recycling should be a priority. Using recycled material almost always consumes less energy than using new materials. Recycling reduces energy needs for mining, refining, and many other manufacturing processes. For example, recycling a pound of steel saves enough energy to light a 60-watt lightbulb for 26 hours. Recycling a ton of glass saves the equivalent of 9 gallons (34 L) of fuel oil. Recycling aluminum cans saves 95% of the energy required to produce aluminum from bauxite. Recycling paper cuts energy usage in half.

Efficiency and conservation are key components of "energy sustainability"—the concept that every generation should meet its energy needs without compromising the energy needs of future generations. Energy sustainability focuses on long-term energy strategies and policies that ensure adequate energy to meet today's needs, as well as tomorrow's. Sustainability also includes investing in research and development of advanced technologies for producing conventional energy sources, promoting the use of alternative energy sources, and encouraging sound environmental policies. The federal government takes these challenges seriously, as they continue necessary research and development on energy efficiency and environmental protection.

Every person can take an active role to help reduce waste at home by learning basic waste-saving habits. Products can be bought that come in concentrated forms or products that use minimal packaging. Most products can be reused, repaired, recycled, or composted instead of simply being thrown away. If every person took part in an energy conservation effort, large quantities of energy resources could be protected and saved for future generations.

CONCLUSION: THE FUTURE OF ENERGY

As illustrated throughout the previous chapters, there are many valuable resources available on Earth that can be used to generate energy. Because the bulk of the energy sources used today are nonrenewable (fossil fuels, uranium, and coal) and will eventually be depleted, it is critical that we look toward developing and maximizing our use of renewable resources. This chapter looks toward the future and what a constantly growing population means to energy consumption. It also examines the greenhouse effect, industries of the future, and emerging technologies. Finally, it addresses the actions each person can take to make a difference and ensure there is enough sustainable energy available for the comfort of future generations.

ENERGY CONSUMPTION AND TRENDS

The U.S. Department of Energy reports that world energy consumption is predicted to increase by 57% from 2002 to 2025. It is not the developed countries that experts believe will be the cause for such an increase in energy use, however. Instead, it is the developing countries of the world. As countries become more developed, they will require much more energy. World oil use is expected to grow from 78 million barrels per day in 2002 to 103 million barrels per day in 2015 and 119 million barrels per day in 2025.

The Middle East (OPEC) countries are expected to be the major suppliers of the increased production that will be required to meet demands. The U.S. Department of Energy has estimated that there are 2,528 billion barrels of oil still left in the Earth.

Natural gas is projected to be the fastest-growing component of world primary energy consumption. World coal consumption is also projected to increase. It is expected to maintain its importance as an energy source in both the electric power and industrial sectors. World net electricity consumption is expected to nearly double. In 2002, 14,275 billion kilowatt-hours were used; in 2015 that number is expected to jump to 21,400 billion kWh; and in 2025 it is expected to reach 26,018 billion kWh, according to the U.S. Department of Energy. Much of the projected growth in renewable electricity generation is expected to result from the completion of large hydroelectric facilities.

THE GREENHOUSE EFFECT

One of the biggest contributors to greenhouse gases is emissions resulting from the burning of fossil fuels. Another greenhouse gas—methane—comes from landfills, coal mines, oil and gas operations, and agriculture. The chemical compounds in the Earth's atmosphere that act as greenhouse gases allow sunlight to enter the atmosphere freely. When sunlight strikes the Earth's surface, some of it is reflected back toward space as heat. Greenhouse gases, however, absorb radiation and trap the heat in the atmosphere. The natural greenhouse effect is a normal function of the Earth's atmosphere. In fact, without it, life could not exist. It is what keeps the Earth warm enough to support life. This natural effect has always been in existence, kept in balance by the Earth's natural processes. The problem with adding additional greenhouse gases through human activity, is that it contributes to global warming, which puts the delicate ecological balance of the Earth at risk. This could cause many disastrous effects, such as flooding or drought.

As more countries become developed and industrialized, more greenhouse gases are released into the atmosphere. This is why this rising level of gases is of extreme concern to scientists. They believe the effects of rising temperatures may produce changes in weather, sea levels, and land use patterns. This, in turn, will lead to climate change on local, regional, and global scales.

World carbon dioxide emissions are expected to increase by 1.9% each year between now and 2025. Developing countries' emissions are expected to grow about the world average at 2.7% annually between now and 2025 and surpass emissions of industrialized countries near 2018.

Scientists are concerned that these results may have a staggering effect on the environment in the long term. In order to control the rising problem with the greenhouse effect, it is important that renewable energy resources continue to be developed and used in order to offset the burning of fossil fuels. Using renewable, sustainable energy will continue to become more critical in order to protect the fragile balance of ecosystems in the future.

INDUSTRIES OF THE FUTURE AND EMERGING TECHNOLOGIES

There are numerous developments in energy research today by the federal government, state governments, educational institutions, and private companies. The specific industrial processes required often determine energy use for industries. For example, the aluminum industry uses large amounts of electricity for smelting, while the glass industry uses large amounts of natural gas to melt silica in furnaces. The nation's eight most energy-intensive industries are aluminum, chemicals, forest products, glass, metal casting, mining, petroleum refining, and steel. Through the development of new technologies, processes are focusing on saving energy and contributing less to pollution by using renewable resources in the U.S. Industrial Technologies Program. The Department of Energy's Industrial Technologies Program has more than 500 research and development programs in progress to address the needs of energy-intensive industries. There are currently 120 technologies that are emerging from research and development and are expected to be ready for commercialization within the next one to two years. Of these, more than 50 have been identified as being immediately ready for field testing. Over the past 24 years, the Industrial Technologies Program has produced over 140 technologies that have successfully been implemented in the marketplace.

In the chemical industry, research is being conducted for several applications, such as chemical synthesis, bioprocesses and biotechnology, process science and engineering, computational technology, and materials. Concerning forest products, research is being done on energy saving and process improvements in wood preparation and raw materials, pulping, bleaching, chemical recovery, papermaking, recycling, recovery, and emission controls. In the glass industry, research projects are looking at saving energy and costs in batch preparation and charging, melting and refining, forming, and finishing.

The petroleum industry is currently working to improve energy and process efficiency, environmental performance, and material and inspection technology. Steel manufacturers are concentrating on projects designed to explore process efficiency, iron unit recycling, environmental engineering, and production efficiency. These technologies have resulted in significant energy savings, waste reduction, increased productivity, lowered emissions, and improved product quality.

Solar Energy

The recent focus of research and development in the solar industry is on increasing the efficiency of, while decreasing the cost of solar cells. A new material is being investigated for its ability to generate electricity from a segment of the solar spectrum that conventional solar cells are unable to use. The electromagnetic energy generated from the sun is enormous. If solar cells can use more of the Sun's electromagnetic energy, then experts believe it will increase the efficiency of solar cells. To reach more of the spectrum, researchers are looking at extremely small particles with semiconducting properties called quantum dots. When the dots are mixed with a polymer that conducts electricity and attaches to electrodes, the result is a solar cell with the ability to generate electricity using the infrared portion of the electromagnetic spectrum.

Coal

The U.S. government and the coal industry are working together to create zero-emission coal gasification power plants. This development is crucial to the future of energy because the United States has vast coal deposits and being able to generate emission-free energy would help control the greenhouse effect. Clean coal technologies include advanced gasifier fuel cells and carbon sequestration. The new gasifiers will be able to convert coal into a gas fuel that can be used to make hydrogen to power fuel cells.

Petroleum

Advanced technologies are also being developed for oil and gas well drilling. The U.S. Department of Energy is working with industries, national laboratories, and universities to develop technologies to reduce the costs and risks of drilling, reduce potential damage to geologic formations, and protect the environment. Advanced drilling technologies will allow geologists to drill faster; drill to deeper depths; drill less expensively; and drill in a cleaner, more environmentally-conscious manner. The ultimate goal is to develop "smart well" technologies that will enable drilling without rigs—systems that will leave no impact on the land. There is also research into advanced drilling systems that anticipate problems and make adjustments automatically. Using lasers for drilling is another focus of the research. Scientists are hopeful that high-power laser technology developed by the U.S. military for national defense could possibly be adapted to drilling for oil and gas.

Transportation

Transportation—because it is such a critical part of a functioning society—is an area that will benefit greatly by energy research and implementation of more environmentally-friendly products. Advanced technology and alternative fuel vehicle research is being done to promote new energy-efficient and renewable energy transportation technologies. Automakers and researchers are continuing to develop and improve on the transportation technologies discovered to date. They are exploring more efficient ways to use fuel cells, alternative fuels, and hybrid-electric vehicles. The hybrid vehicles available today on the market are gaining in popularity as people take positive steps to switch to this new type of transportation. Scientists are also working on new ways to store energy and create lightweight, advanced materials to make vehicles that run cleaner and use less fuel.

In addition to the technologies available now, according to the Department of Energy, researchers across the United States are developing new advanced technologies for use in cars, minivans, pickup trucks, sports utility vehicles, buses, and heavy-duty trucks that will create an even cleaner future with more available domestic fuel resources. Non-petroleum-based fuels and fuel components will probably come from nonfossil sources such as biomass, vegetable oils, and waste animal fats, as well as from fossil sources other than crude oil, such as tar sands and oil shale.

Researchers have also identified options for replacing some of the petroleum fuels used in transportation vehicles with fuels made from domestic renewable sources. This "biomass-derived fuel" can be made from a variety of organic materials—trees, plants and plant residues, plant fiber, poultry litter and other animal wastes, industrial waste, and the paper component of municipal solid waste.

Advanced materials—such as metals, polymers, composites, and intermetallic compounds—also play an important role in improving the efficiency of transportation engines and vehicles. Weight reduction is one of the most practical ways to increase the fuel economy of vehicles while reducing exhaust emissions. The less a car weighs, the better mileage efficiency it can achieve.

The use of lightweight, high-performance materials will contribute to the development of vehicles that provide better fuel economy but are comparable in size, comfort, and safety to today's vehicles. This way, making the change to increase energy efficiency will not impact the level of comfort previously enjoyed. The development of propulsion

Biomass energy sources will become more important in the future as energy sources other than fossil fuel are sought. (a) These hybrid poplar trees in Oregon are harvested for fiber and fuel. Once the trees are cut, they are chipped into smaller pieces and used to generate power. (b) This is a biomass research farm operated by the State University of New York College of Environmental Science and Forestry. A patchwork quilt of willow and poplar plots are grown and tested for future energy potential. *(a, National Renewable Energy Laboratory, photo by Warren Gretz; b, National Renewable Energy Laboratory, photo by Lawrence P. Abrahamson)*

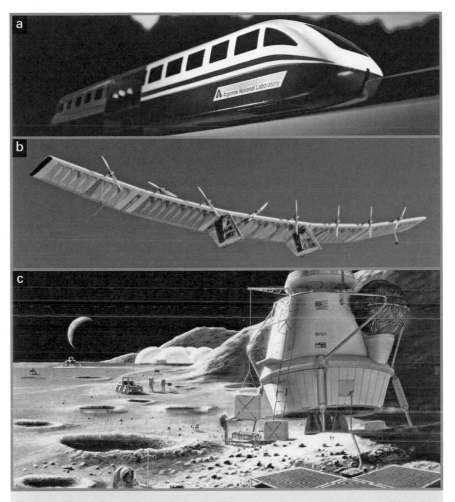

Future applications of energy: (a) Vehicles like this model may be available in the future. They are sleek tubes that will transport travelers at 300 mph (483 km/h), levitating inches over powerful magnetic fields created by on-board superconducting magnets. Argonne National Laboratory in Illinois is currently testing this system. (b) This unmanned craft weighs 430 pounds (195 kg) and has eight electric motor propellers powered by the sun. The aircraft is being designed for use by the Ballistic Missile Defense Organization. (c) NASA is focusing on using new energy sources for future space exploration. Seen above is an illustration of a Mars excursion vehicle that may one day be used for human space exploration. *(a, b, courtesy of Department of Energy; c, courtesy of NASA, illustrated by Pat Rawlings)*

materials and technologies will help reduce costs while improving the durability and efficiency of advanced internal combustion, diesel, hybrid, and fuel-cell-powered vehicles.

Home Automation

As home automation technology becomes more developed, it will save significant amounts of energy. Direct savings will come from automatic shut-off features and occupancy sensors. Occupancy sensor technologies save the automated-house owner energy and money by limiting lighting, appliance, and space-conditioning use when rooms or zones are unoccupied for a certain length of time (this is already a practice in effect today for many government and business offices). Photosensors adjust the lighting in a room to take advantage of daylight. When tied to a home-automation system, the heating, cooling, and ventilation systems (HVAC) can be adjusted to account for passive solar heat gains. Systems connected to a home-automation system can also be turned on remotely by telephone, so systems can be set making the home comfortable when the owner arrives.

Another component of home-automation systems in the future will be load shifting and management. Many "smart" appliances, as discussed previously, are programmable so that homeowners can take advantage of lower utility rates at times when utility demand is low. In the future, houses with home automation will be able to "communicate" with utilities so that certain appliances—washers, water heaters, heating, ventilation, and cooling—are automatically deactivated during the peak demand periods, thereby saving energy and strain on the energy infrastructure, such as transformers and generators.

Another feature to expect in the future is an option for "staged power return" after blackouts. It requires a lot of energy for utilities to restart a power plant after a power failure, especially in the summer when many air conditioners run continuously. With warm temperatures, the system is already taxed, but when thousands of appliances must be started up at once, it stresses the system even more. With a staged return of power, utilities can control the rate at which power returns after a blackout, first sending electricity to essential home appliances—such as furnaces, refrigerators, and freezers—and then sending it to the remaining appliances.

Thermal storage is also a concept that researchers have been planning for the future. Heat that is generated by conventional or renewable means during off-peak hours can be stored in ceramic bricks, water, or other storage materials. Release of the thermal energy could be controlled by computers.

Energy—heat and cooling—will also become "zoned" and "programmable." Programmable thermostats can control the temperature on a room-by-room basis, instead of the whole house. That way, only rooms currently being used would have their temperature controlled. Based on information from the Department of Energy, in one high-tech application, people carry sensors that are programmed to their personal preferences. The system reads these when people enter a room and adjusts the indoor environment accordingly.

The monitoring of air quality is another future application. Home-automation systems could control the ventilation system to operate only when the house is occupied. Additional sensors could control a room's humidity.

Geothermal Energy

Steam and hot water reservoirs are just a small part of the geothermal resources. The Earth's magma and hot, dry rock is expected to provide cheap, clean, and almost unlimited energy as soon as the technology is developed to use it. As new discoveries are made in the current technology, engineers will be able to drill to deeper depths to access additional energy sources.

Fuel Cells and Hydrogen

Fuel cells are a promising technology for use as a source of heat and electricity in buildings and as an electrical power source for vehicles. Auto companies are working on building cars and trucks that use fuel cells. Scientists expect that hydrogen, as a nearly ideal energy carrier, will play a critical role in providing power to vehicles, homes, and industries. It is nontoxic, renewable, and clean to use. It is the fuel of choice for energy-efficient fuel cells. If, in the future, hydrogen is produced from water and powered by renewable energy, the energy life cycle of hydrogen will be entirely pollution free.

Before hydrogen becomes a significant fuel in the U.S. energy picture, many new systems must be built. For example, systems will need to be built that can make, store, and move hydrogen. Pipelines and economical fuel cells will also be necessary. The good news is that fuel cells are becoming more affordable. Automakers are experimenting with fuel cells that extract hydrogen from gasoline or methanol (an alcohol made from natural gas). In addition, consumers will need the technology and the education with which to use it.

The goal of the U.S. Department of Energy's Hydrogen Program is for hydrogen to produce 10% of the nation's energy by the year 2030. Hydrogen could provide clean, renewable energy for the future. One suggestion for energy in the future is to put huge solar power satellites into orbit around the Earth. They would collect solar energy from the Sun, convert it to electricity, and beam it to Earth as microwaves or some other form of transmission. The positive side is that the power would have no greenhouse gas emissions, but some people fear microwave beams might cause health problems. According to current research, these satellites may not be practical for another century, if at all.

Communication Satellites

The nature of future satellite communications systems will depend on the demands of the marketplace—such as direct home distribution of entertainment, data transfers between businesses, telephone traffic, and cellular phone traffic. It will also depend on the costs of making and launching the satellites and the design of fiber optic cables that make communication possible.

One approach that is currently being tested experimentally is the "switchboard in the sky" concept. This concept would make it possible to control a multitude of uplink and downlink beams by a steerable method—the beams could be moved to different parts of the Earth within milliseconds. NASA's Advanced Communications Technology Satellite (ACTS) is one of the first systems to demonstrate and test high frequencies for satellite communications.

Wind Power

Wind power will continue to grow as people become more concerned about the greenhouse effect and pollution. Many electric utility customers currently take advantage of the "green" energy option to use electricity generated by wind power when it is offered by their public utility company; this trend is increasing. One of the drawbacks of wind power in the past was its cost. But now, electricity from the best wind turbines is as cheap as electricity from a coal-fired power plant. Researchers believe that wind power can be reduced to half of its current cost by using lightweight composite materials, better computerized control systems, and more efficient generators.

POWER FOR THE NEXT GENERATION

Besides technology, people's attitudes are also important to the future use of energy—in fact, attitudes may well be one of the most important components to the overall success of future energy-saving technologies. With the costs of using renewable energy becoming more affordable, Americans are becoming increasingly supportive of nonpolluting power. Also important is the concept of the "three Rs"—reduce, reuse, and recycle. In addition to lessening landfill waste and conserving natural resources, following the three Rs decreases pollution by reducing the need to manufacture, distribute, and use materials from raw resources.

Curbside recycling programs currently serve about half of the U.S. population. Some communities even have "pay as you throw" programs, with waste collection fees based on the amount thrown away—which presents a direct economic incentive for people to generate less waste. Today, the United States recycles 28% of its waste, almost double the level of 15 years ago. Recycling of specific materials, such as aluminum, has grown even more. Purchasing recycled materials closes the recycling loop and makes recycling programs successful.

In addition to recycling, if people become more energy conscious and energy conservative—such as using efficient lighting, insulating homes, driving less often or carpooling, and using other methods that have been discussed in previous chapters—energy will be available for people now and well into the future. This concept of sustainable energy makes it possible to also protect the environment and be responsible stewards of the land.

MAKING A DIFFERENCE

Fortunately, we are also presented with vast opportunities to make a difference today. Studying and working with energy sources can help us develop a new sensitivity to the flow of energy in the world around us and a deeper appreciation for the role energy plays in each of our lives.

There are almost limitless possibilities for scientific exploration and innovation in the fields of energy technology, energy efficiency, and conservation, especially as applied to renewable and alternative energy resources. Trends to date indicate a positive step in developing a more energy efficient tomorrow. To make sure we have plenty of energy in the future, it is up to everyone to use energy wisely. Everyone must conserve energy and use it efficiently. All energy sources have an impact on the environment. Of all the Earth's precious resources, no other resource has contributed to the development and advancement of civilization in the way that energy has. As we have seen throughout this book, the rapid technological developments that have occurred over the past two decades alone have had a tremendous effect on our quality of life. With new sources of energy being tapped, we are only limited by our imaginations.

SIGNIFICANT EVENTS IN THE HISTORY OF ENERGY BY FUEL

Wood (Biomass)

Pre-1885 Wood was the primary source for cooking, warmth, light, trains, and steamboats; cutting wood was time-consuming, hard work.

Electricity

1700s After eons of superstitious imaginations about electricity, Ben Franklin figured out that static electricity and lightning were the same; his correct understanding of the nature of electricity paved the way for the future.

1830–1839 Michael Faraday built an induction dynamo based on principles of electromagnetism, induction, generation, and transmission.

1860s Mathematical theory of electromagnetic fields was published; Maxwell created a new era of physics when he unified magnetism, electricity, and light; one of the most significant events, possibly the very most significant event, of the nineteenth century was Maxwell's discovery of the four laws of electrodynamics ("Maxwell's Equations"), which led to electric power, radios, and television.

Coal

1763–1774 Pumping water from coal mines was a most difficult and expensive problem; the steam engine developed by James Watt during these years provided the solution; Watt's steam engine remained basically unchanged for the next century, and its uses expanded to change the whole nature of industry and transportation.

1885–1950 Coal was the most important fuel; one-half ton of coal produced as much energy as 2 tons of wood and at half the cost, but it was hard to stay clean in houses heated with coal.

Late 1860s The steel industry gave coal a big boost.

1982 Coal accounted for more than half of the supply of electricity, but little was used in homes; in terms of national electricity generation, hydropower, natural gas, and nuclear energy contributed between 10% and 15% each.

Oil

1870 Oil had become the country's second biggest export after Edwin Drake started the industry.

1890 Mass production of automobiles began, creating demand for gasoline; prior to this, kerosene used for lighting had been the main oil product.

1951–present Oil has given us most of our energy; automobiles increased the demand for oil.

1960 The Organization of Petroleum Exporting Countries (OPEC) was formed by Iran, Iraq, Kuwait, Saudi Arabia, and Venezuela; the group has since grown to include 11 member countries.

1970 U.S. production of petroleum (crude oil and natural gas plant liquids) reached its highest level at 11.7 million barrels per day; production in the lower 48 states has been generally declining since 1970; some of this decline has been offset by increased Alaskan production after 1978.

1993   For the first time, the United States imported more oil and refined products from other countries than it produced. This trend continues today.

Nuclear

1906   Albert Einstein discovered the special theory of relativity, which unified mass, energy, magnetism, electricity, and light with the equation $E = mc^2$ (energy = mass times the square of the speed of light); this led to nuclear medicine—and a much longer life span—astrophysics, and commercial nuclear electric power.

1942   Scientists produced nuclear energy in a sustained nuclear reaction.

1957   The first commercial nuclear power plant began operating.

1995   Nuclear power contributed about 20% of the nation's electricity.

Ethanol

1826   Samuel Morey developed an engine that ran on ethanol and turpentine.

1860   German engine inventor Nicholas Otto used ethanol as the fuel in one of his engines; Otto is best known for his development of a modern internal combustion engine (the Otto Cycle) in 1876.

1917–1918   The need for fuel during World War I drove up the ethanol demand to 50–60 million gallons (189–227 million liters) per year.

1920s   Gasoline became the motor fuel of choice; Standard Oil began adding ethanol to gasoline to increase octane and reduce engine knocking.

1930s Fuel ethanol gained a market in the Midwest; more than 2,000 gasoline stations in the Midwest sold gasohol, which was gasoline blended with between 6% and 12% ethanol.

1945–1978 Once World War II ended, with reduced need for war materials and with the low price of fuel, ethanol use as a fuel was drastically reduced; from the late 1940s until the late 1970s, virtually no commercial fuel ethanol was available anywhere in the United States.

1975 The United States begins to phase out lead in gasoline; ethanol becomes more attractive as a possible octane booster for gasoline; the Environmental Protection Agency (EPA) issued the initial regulations requiring reduced levels of lead in gasoline in early 1973; by 1986, no lead was to be allowed in motor gasoline.

1979 Marketing of commercial alcohol-blended fuels began; Amoco Oil Company began marketing commercial alcohol-blended fuels, followed by Ashland, Chevron, Beacon, and Texaco.

1979 Congress enacted a series of tax benefits to ethanol producers and blenders; these benefits encouraged the growth of ethanol production.

1988 Ethanol was first used as an oxygenate in gasoline; Denver, Colorado, mandated oxygenated fuels (fuels containing oxygen) for winter use to control carbon monoxide emissions.

1992 The Energy Policy Act of 1992 (EPACT) provided for two additional gasoline blends—7.7% and 5.7% ethanol, respectively.

Geothermal

1900s Conversion of high-grade hydrothermal resources to electricity began in Italy.

1960   The first commercial-scale development tools were placed in California at The Geysers, a 10-megawatt unit owned by Pacific Gas & Electric.

1972   Deep well drilling technology improvements led to deeper reservoir drilling and access to more resources.

1977   Hot dry rock was demonstrated in 1977; scientists developed the first hot dry rock reservoir at Fenton Hill, New Mexico.

1978   U.S. Department of Energy (DOE) funding for geothermal research and development was $106.2 million in fiscal year 1978, marking the first time the funding level surpassed $100 million; it remained at more than $100 million until fiscal year 1982, when it was reduced to $56.4 million.

1982   Geothermal electric generating capacity, primarily utility-owned, reached a new high level of 1,000 megawatts.

1988   U.S. Department of Energy and the Electric Power Research Institute operated a 1-megawatt geopressured power demonstration plant in Texas, extracting methane and heat from brine liquids.

1994   California Energy became the world's largest geothermal company through its acquisition of Magma Power; near-term international markets gained the interest of U.S. geothermal developers.

1995   During the period 1985–1995, U.S. geothermal developers had added nearly 1,000 megawatts of geothermal electric generating capacity outside The Geysers; worldwide geothermal capacity reached 6,000 megawatts.

Source: U.S. Department of Energy

absorption   The process of soaking up energy that has been received by radiation, often sunlight.

acid rain   Rain that becomes slightly acidic because it mixes with polluting gases in the atmosphere. Acid rain can eventually kill trees.

aerogenerator   A wind turbine used to produce electricity.

alternative energy   Energy produced using methods such as wind power or solar power, which can cause less pollution than traditional methods and relies on sources that can be used again and again (renewable sources).

alternator   An electricity generator used by cars and other vehicles.

anthracite   A hard, natural coal that is rich in carbon. Coal in its anthracite stage is very old. It burns slowly, giving off great heat, and leaves no ashes.

atmosphere   The shell of gases that surrounds the Earth. There are several layers to the atmosphere. The one closest to the ground, called the troposphere, is where clouds form; above it is the stratosphere, the region of thin air containing the gas ozone that helps to shield animals and plants from levels of ultraviolet radiation that are too high.

atom   The smallest particle that makes up one of the 118 known pure substances, or elements, in the universe.

battery   A store of chemicals that release their energy as electricity when connected to an electric circuit.

biomass energy   Changing farming wastes, grasses, trees, bark, sawdust, and other things into energy by burning them, changing them into a gas, or converting them to liquid fuel.

bituminous coal   A word used to describe the character of soft black coal that burns with a smoky yellow flame.

carbohydrate   A group of substances that includes a number of sugar-making chemicals, of which the most important is starch.

carbon dioxide   Burning fossil fuels releases carbon that has been stored underground for millions of years into the atmosphere. The carbon in these fossil fuels is transformed into carbon dioxide, the predominant gas contributing to the greenhouse effect, during the combustion process. While carbon dioxide is absorbed and released at nearly equal rates by natural processes on the Earth, this equilibrium may be disrupted when large amounts of carbon dioxide are released into the atmosphere by human activities, such as the burning of fossil fuels.

carbon monoxide   Carbon monoxide is a colorless, odorless gas resulting from the incomplete combustion of hydrocarbon fuels. Carbon monoxide interferes with the blood's ability to carry oxygen to the body's tissues and results in numerous adverse health effects, including death.

chemical energy   The energy stored in chemicals that can be released when the chemical takes part in a chemical reaction.

coal   Coal is formed from plant and animal matter that has been subjected to geologic heat and pressure, transformed over millions of years into hard black solids. Because coal is a readily available resource in the United States, coal power plants provide about half of the nation's electricity. However, coal-fired power plants generally cause more pollution per unit of electricity than any other fuel. Most coal plants are required to have several pollution control devices to reduce the amount of pollutants that are released into the air from burning the coal.

conduction   The movement of heat through solid objects. The energy is passed from atom to atom.

conductor   A material that allows electricity or heat to flow through it easily.

conserve   To protect and use wisely so that a resource will not be exhausted. Conserving fossil fuels is one of the biggest challenges facing the world today.

control rods   Long metal rods that control the fission process within the reactor core. The position of the rods determines the speed at which fission occurs.

convection   The process of circulating heat through liquids and gases that is brought about because warm liquids and gases become lighter and rise, while cool ones become denser and sink.

coolant substances   Substances used in a nuclear reactor to absorb the heat created by fission. Water is often used as a coolant.

cooling towers   Places where water that has been used in the power station is cooled down.

core   The "heart" of a nuclear power plant containing the uranium (or other nuclear fuel). Fission takes place within the core.

current   A flow of electric charge, made up of electrons moving inside an electrical conductor.

derrick   A framework erected over a drilled hole, which is used to support the drilling equipment. Derricks are often used in drilling for oil.

dioxins   Dioxins are man-made chemical compounds that enter the air through fuel and waste emissions, including motor vehicle exhaust fumes and garbage incineration. Skin rashes, liver damage, weight loss, and a reduction in the effectiveness of the immune system have all been attributed to human exposure to dioxins.

elastic energy   The energy stored in a squashed, stretched, or bent elastic object.

electric circuit   A loop of material that conducts electricity that an electric current can flow around.

electrical energy   The energy carried by an electric current flowing around a circuit.

electromagnetic spectrum   A family of waves, including light, radio waves, microwaves, infrared rays, and X-rays.

electron   A small, negatively charged particle circling the nucleus of an atom.

energy   The ability to do work.

energy converter   A device used to change energy from one form into another. Converters can be very simple devices such as a waterwheel blade, or they can be complex devices such as steam or electrical engines.

energy crops   Crops grown specifically for their fuel value, including food crops such as corn and sugarcane, and nonfood crops such as poplar trees and switchgrass.

energy efficiency   Energy efficiency refers to products or systems using less energy to do the same or better job than conventional products or systems. Energy efficiency saves energy, saves money on utility bills, and helps protect the environment by reducing the amount of electricity that needs to be generated.

evaporation   The process whereby moisture is lost from the surface of plants, the ground, and the oceans. The energy to change liquid water into moisture comes from the Sun, which is why the ground dries more quickly on a warm summer's day than on a cold winter's day.

fantail   A small wheel or vane to one side of a windmill, used to turn the windmill into the wind automatically.

fat   A substance that the body makes to store energy. It is one of the body's main sources of fuel.

fission   The process whereby the energy in radioactive substances such as plutonium and uranium is rapidly released to make heat.

fossil fuels   Energy sources formed by the decay of plants, dinosaurs, and other animals over millions of years; coal, oil, and natural gas are fossil fuels.

fuel   A concentrated form of energy that is burned as a source of heat or power.

fusion   A type of nuclear reaction that uses the atoms of light elements. In fusion, the nuclei of two lighter atoms combine—or fuse—to form a third, heavier nucleus. The Sun's energy is released through fusion.

generator   A machine in which movement energy is converted to electricity.

geothermal energy   Using the heat from the Earth to produce power.

geyser   A naturally occurring, intermittent fountain of water that occurs in some places where the rocks below the surface are still hot.

global climate change   Global climate change could result in sea-level rises, changes to patterns of precipitation, increased variability in the weather, and a variety of other consequences. These changes threaten our health, agriculture, water resources, forests, wildlife, and coastal areas.

gravitational energy   The potential energy that an object has because of its position in a gravitational field.

green power   Electricity that is generated from renewable energy sources is often referred to as "green power." Green power products can include electricity generated exclusively from renewable resources or, more frequently, electricity produced from a combination of fossil and renewable resources.

greenhouse effect   The process by which the atmosphere helps trap the sun's heat. Like the glass of a greenhouse, the Earth's atmosphere allows sunlight through to the Earth's surface. The light warms the Earth, but the heat it creates cannot easily pass through the atmosphere and escape into space. This trapped heat warms the Earth. Pollutants can increase the greenhouse effect, possibly causing climatic change.

heat energy   The energy that an object has because of its temperature. Hotter, larger objects have more heat energy.

hydropower   Using the energy in flowing water to make electricity.

impermeable   Not permitting passage of a fluid, or other material, through a substance.

impurities   Materials of an inferior or worthless quality that are mixed with more valuable materials.

insulation   Material used to stop electricity or heat from escaping.

insulator   A material that does not allow electricity or heat to flow through it.

joule (J)   The SI unit of energy.

kinetic energy   The energy that an object has because it is moving or spinning around.

kilowatt (kW)   Equal to 1,000 watts, a measure of electrical power.

kilowatt-hour (kWh)   A unit of energy equivalent to 1,000 watts of electrical power being used for one hour.

light energy   The energy carried from place to place in rays of light.

light water reactor   A nuclear reactor that uses water as both its coolant substance and its moderator. Many reactors in the United States are of this type.

lignite   A brownish black coal between the peat and bituminous coal stages. Lignite is loose-grained and does not heat as well as later coal forms.

magnetic field   The region around a magnet where its magnetic effect can be felt.

megawatt (MW)   Equal to 1 million watts, a measure of electrical power.

meter   A machine that measures something.

moderator   A material used to increase the chances of fission. A moderator slows down the neutrons that pass through it, allowing them to split atoms.

molecule   The simplest structural unit formed when two or more different atoms join together.

municipal solid waste   Using trash or garbage to produce energy by burning it or by capturing the gases it gives off and using them as fuel.

natural gas   Natural gas is a fossil fuel formed when layers of buried plants and animals decompose over a long period of time. The energy that the plants and animals originally obtained from the Sun is stored in the natural gas. The primary component of natural gas is methane, a potent greenhouse gas. Natural gas is a nonrenewable resource.

neutron   One of two kinds of particles found in the nucleus of an atom. The neutron is an electrically neutral particle.

nonrenewable fuels   Fuels that cannot be easily made or "renewed." Oil, natural gas, and coal are nonrenewable fuels.

nuclear energy   The energy stored inside an atom, which is released when the atom's nucleus splits up or combines with another nucleus.

nuclear reaction   A process by which the structure of an atom's nucleus is changed. Fission, fusion, and radioactive decay are three major forms of nuclear reactions.

nuclear reactor   A device in which nuclear reactions can be created and controlled for the purpose of creating nuclear energy.

nucleus   The core of an atom, usually consisting of particles known as protons and neutrons.

oil   Oil is a liquid fossil fuel that is formed from layers of buried plants and animals that have been subjected to geologic heat and pressure over a long period of time. The energy that the plants and animals originally obtained from the sun is stored in the oil in the form of carbon. In addition to carbon, oil contains elements such as nitrogen, sulfur, mercury, lead, and arsenic. Oil is a nonrenewable resource.

ore   A mineral or rock from which a valuable substance, such as metal, is derived.

passive solar heater   A solar water-heating or space-heating system that moves heated air or water without using pumps or fans.

passive solar home   A house that uses a room or another part of the building as a solar collector.

peat   Partially carbonized vegetable matter. Peat is considered to be the first stage in the formation of coal.

petroleum   The general name for the gases and liquid fuels that form in the rocks over millions of years. Gasoline is just one refined component of petroleum.

photon   A tiny "bundle" of energy radiated by the Sun.

photosynthesis   The process that plants use whereby they absorb the energy from the Sun in order to build their tissues.

photovoltaic energy   A type of solar energy that converts sunshine into electricity.

pollution   The release of unnatural quantities of materials into the environment so as to disrupt the normal life processes. Levels of pollutants, such as metals in rivers or acid gases in the air, have built up to dangerous proportions in some parts of the world.

potential energy   Energy that can be released by an object or a substance, such as gravitational energy, elastic energy, or chemical energy.

power   The rate at which energy is converted from one form to another.

power station   A place where electricity is made.

prospecting   Exploring an area, especially for mineral deposits.

proton   One of two types of particles found in the nucleus of an atom. Protons have a positive charge.

pylons   Tall, metal towers used to carry power lines.

radiate   One of the ways that heat is transferred. The Sun's heat is radiated through space in the form of photons. The atmosphere, the land, and the oceans then absorb these photons.

radioactive   A word used to describe a substance that gives out energy in the form of radiation.

radioactive decay   A natural nuclear reaction by which an atom's nucleus changes into the nucleus of another. The change releases energy in the form of particles and rays (nuclear radiation).

refine   To separate out the components of a liquid such as crude oil in order to make the raw material more useful.

refinery   An industrial plant where crude substances, especially petroleum, are purified.

renewable energy   Types of energy that are "renewed" as we use them; solar, wind, and geothermal energy are forms of renewable energy.

rotor   A set of blades attached to a central hub so that they can rotate.

sediment   The material that settles out at the bottom of an ocean, river, or lake and that is made of fine fragments of rock eroded from the land. Sediments eventually become crushed into new rocks, which are then called sedimentary rocks.

SI unit   A unit of measurement in the SI System of Units (Système International d'Unités), which is used by scientists in most parts of the world.

slag heaps   Hills of leftover materials from mining operations.

smelt   To melt or fuse ores in order to extract the metals contained in them.

solar cell   A device for converting sunlight into electricity.

solar collectors   Boxes, frames, or rooms that trap the sun's rays to produce heat.

solar energy   Energy given off by the Sun. This energy is produced by nuclear reactions that occur at the Sun's core.

solar heating   Using the Sun's energy to heat homes and water.

solar panel   Flat, doorlike panels that soak up the Sun's energy and use it to heat water or make electricity.

sound energy   Vibrations that travel through the particles of air, liquids, or solids and that carry energy with them.

spectrum   The wide range of colors that make up visible light.

strip mining   An open form of mining in which the coal seams run close to ground level and are exposed by the stripping of the topsoil.

sulfur dioxide   High concentrations of sulfur dioxide affect breathing and may aggravate existing respiratory and cardiovascular disease. Sulfur dioxide is a primary contributor to acid rain, which causes acidification of lakes and streams and can damage trees, crops, historic buildings, and statues. Sulfur dioxide is released primarily from burning fuels that contain sulfur (such as coal, oil, and diesel fuel). Stationary sources such as coal- and oil-fired power plants, steel mills, refineries, pulp and paper mills, and nonferrous smelters are the largest releasers.

temperature   A measure of how hot an object is. Adding heat energy to an object increases its temperature.

thermometer   An instrument used for measuring temperature.

turbine   A fan-shaped engine used to produce electricity.

ultraviolet   An invisible part of the radiation sent out in all directions by the sun. High levels of ultraviolet radiation are harmful for most plants and animals.

vacuum   A space that contains nothing, including air.

voltage   The potential energy that pushes a current around an electric circuit.

water cycle   The continuous process whereby water is evaporated from oceans and other wet surfaces, rises through the air as moisture to form clouds, and is then returned to the ground as rain or snow before flowing as rivers back to the oceans.

watt (W)   The SI unit of power, equal to one joule per second.

wind farms   Groups of dozens to thousands of wind turbines that produce large amounts of electricity.

wind power   Using the wind to produce electricity by turning blades on a wind turbine.

wind power plant   A group of wind turbines interconnected to a common utility system.

windmill   A building with wind-driven sails that turn a millstone to grind grain into flour. Also a wind-driven pump.

work   The result of force moving an object, measured in joules.

Amdur, Richard. *The Fragile Earth.* New York: Chelsea House Publishers, 1994.

Arnold, Guy. *Facts on Water, Wind, and Solar Power.* New York: Franklin Watts Publisher, 1990.

Brown, Warren. *Alternative Sources of Energy.* New York: Chelsea House Publishers, 1994.

Bryant-Mole, Karen. *Electricity.* Crystal Lake, Ill.: Rigby Interactive Library, 1997.

Carless, Jennifer. *Renewable Energy: A Concise Guide to Green Alternatives.* New York: Walker and Co., 1993.

Challoner, Jack. *Energy.* New York: Dorling Kindersley Publishing Inc., 1993.

Fowler, Allan. *Energy From the Sun.* New York: Children's Press, 1997.

Gardner, Robert. *Energy Projects for Young Scientists.* New York: Franklin Watts, 1987.

Graham, Ian. *Wind Power.* New York: Raintree Steck-Vaughn Publishers, 1999.

Herda, D. J. *Energy Resources: Toward a Renewable Future.* New York: Franklin Watts, 1991.

Johnstone, Hugh. *Facts on Future Energy Possibilities.* New York: Franklin Watts Publisher, 1990.

Keeler, Barbara. *Energy Alternatives.* Chicago: Lucent Books, 1990.

Knapp, Brian. *Science in Our World: Energy.* Danbury, Conn.: Grolier Educational Corporation, 1992.

Lafferty, Peter. *The World of Science.* New York: Facts on File, 1994.

Litvinoff, Miles. *Raw Materials.* New York: Heinemann Library, 1996.

Oxlade, Chris. *Energy.* Des Plaines, Ill.: Heinemann Library Publishing, 1999.

Pack, Janet. *Fueling the Future.* New York: Children's Press, 1992.

Petersen, Christine. *Water Power.* New York: Scholastic Inc., 2004.

_____. *Wind Power.* New York: Scholastic Inc., 2004.

Riley, Peter D. *Energy.* New York: Heinemann Library, 1998.

Rybolt, Thomas R., and Robert C. Mebane. *Environmental Experiments About Renewable Energy.* Hillside, N. J.: Enslow Publishers Inc., 1994.

Taylor, Barbara. *Energy and Power.* New York: Franklin Watts, 1990.

Walker, John F. *Wind Energy Technology.* Norman, Okla.: University of Oklahoma Press, 1997.

Ward, Alan. *Experimenting With Energy.* New York: Chelsea House Publishers, 1994.

Yanda, Bill. *Rads, Ergs, & Cheeseburgers: The Kid's Guide to Energy & the Environment.* Southampton, Mass.: J. Muir Publications, 1991.

WEB SITES

Association for the Conservation of Energy
http://www.ukace.org

Energy Conservation
http://www.nps.gov/renew/conservation.htm

Energy Information Association
http://www.cia.doc.gov

Energy Quest
http://www.energyquest.ca.qov

Energy Star
http://www.energystar.gov

Home Energy
http://www.homeenergy.org

Home Energy Saver
http://hes.lbl.gov

Lawrence Livermore National Laboratory
http://www.llnl.gov

National Energy Conservation Association
http://www.neca.ca

Public Housing Energy Conservation Clearinghouse
http://www.hud.gov/offices/pih/programs/ph/phecc

SLAC Energy Conservation
http://www.slac.stanford.edu/slac/energy

U.S. Department of Energy
http://www.doe.gov/forstudentsandkids.htm

U.S. Department of Energy, Energy Efficiency and Renewable Energy
http://www1.eere.energy.gov

JULIE KERR CASPER holds B.S., M.S., and Ph.D. degrees in earth science with an emphasis on natural resource conservation. She has worked for the United States Bureau of Land Management (BLM) for nearly 30 years and is primarily focused on practical issues concerning the promotion of a healthier, better-managed environment for both the short- and long-term. She has also had extensive experience teaching middle school and high school students over the past 20 years. She has taught classes, instructed workshops, given presentations, and led field trips and science application exercises. She is also the author of several award-winning novels, articles, and stories.